The

# Year

of the

# Poet VII

## November 2020

**The Poetry Posse**

inner child press, ltd.

# The Poetry Posse 2020

Gail Weston Shazor

Shareef Abdur Rasheed

Teresa E. Gallion

hülya n. yılmaz

Kimberly Burnham

Tzemin Ition Tsai

Elizabeth Esguerra Castillo

Jackie Davis Allen

Joe Paire

Caroline 'Ceri' Nazareno

Ashok K. Bhargava

Alicja Maria Kuberska

Swapna Behera

Albert 'Infinite' Carrasco

Eliza Segiet

William S. Peters, Sr.

~ * ~

In order to maintain each poet's authentic voice, this volume has not undergone the scrutiny of editing. Please take time to indulge each contributor for their own creativity and aspirations to convey their uniqueness.

hülya n. yılmaz, Ph.D.
Director of Editing ~
Inner Child Press International

# The Year of the Poet VII
## November 2020 Edition

## The Poetry Posse

### 1st Edition : 2020

### Publisher Information
#### 1st Edition : Inner Child Press
#### intouch@innerchildpress.com
#### www.innerchildpress.com

ISBN-13 : 978-1-952081-33-0 (inner child press, ltd.)

$ 12.99

# WHAT WOULD LIFE BE WITHOUT A LITTLE POETRY?

# Dedication

This Book is dedicated to

## Humanity, Peace & Poetry

the Power of the Pen

can effectuate change!

&

## The Poetry Posse

past, present & future

our Patrons and Readers

the Spirit of our Everlasting Muse

*In the darkness of my life*
*I heard the music*
*I danced . . .*
*and the Light appeared*
*and I dance*

Janet P. Caldwell

# Table of Contents

# The Poetry Posse

# Table of Contents . . . *continued*

# November's Featured Poets     107

# Foreword

*Tyranny Is Not Terrible, What Is Terrible Is Submission, Silence Or Praise To Tyranny*

~ Liu Xiaobo

On December 28, 1955, six years after the Communist Party of China established its regime, Liu Xiaobo was born into an intellectual family in Changchun City, Jilin Province. That was the era as China's "the Great Proletarian Cultural Revolution" emerged.

Regarding the Cultural Revolution, Liu Xiaobo recalled: "I am very grateful for the Great Proletarian Cultural Revolution. I was a kid at that time and I could do whatever I wanted." "Schools were closed, and I could temporarily get rid of the education process, do what I want, and play. Go to war, I had a great time."

Beginning in 1984, for several consecutive years, Liu Xiaobo published "On Artistic Intuition", "A New Aesthetic Trend", "Inevitable Reflection- Talking from Several Novels About Intellectuals", "Crisis! Literature in the new era is facing a crisis!", Let the "Liu Xiaobo Phenomenon" that shook the literary world first show its brilliance and arouse repercussions among young students.

Liu Xiaobo developed from literary criticism to ideological and cultural criticism, and became the spokesperson of irrationalism and anti-traditional thoughts. In 1987, Liu Xiaobo published his famous work "A Critique of Choice—A Dialogue with Li Zehou" and in 1988, after publishing his doctoral dissertation "Aesthetics and Human Freedom", he became a Ph.D. in literature and applied for a lecturer in the Chinese Department of Beijing Normal University. After all, he surrendered to the educational program system which he opposed throughout his life.

On April 15, 1989, the former General Secretary of the Communist Party of China Hu Yaobang passed away. Colleges and universities in Beijing and across the country held mourning activities, and even developed into a large-scale street protest movement. Liu Xiaobo immediately responded and participated in the support activities of overseas Chinese students and visiting scholars.

On April 20th, Liu Xiaobo issued a "Reform Proposal" urging the Chinese Communist Party to reflect on and correct its mistakes, requesting a re-examination of the issues related to the 1983 "Clear Spiritual Pollution" movement and the 1987 "Anti-Bourgeois Liberalization" movement, and advocated the protection of basic human rights Articles, open private newspapers, prohibit convictions for words, and truly implement freedom of speech, freedom of the press and freedom of the press.

On April 22, Liu Xiaobo published "Reflections on Hu Yaobang's Death Phenomenon" in the "World Journal", drafting an "Open Letter to Chinese University Students", criticizing China's socialist system as an "autocratic regime". He tried to find a way to reform China from the system.

However, in the June 4th Tiananmen Incident that broke out on June 4, 1989, Liu Xiaobo was arrested for participating in student movement activities and was forced to "testify" on CCTV that he "has not seen the army kill people on Tiananmen Square." What is embarrassing is that he still can't escape the end of being expelled from public office after all.

On October 10, 1996, Liu Xiaobo issued the "Double Ten Declaration", discussing the political basis of cross-strait reunification, the Tibet issue, the issue of improving the National People's Congress system, and the Diaoyu Islands issue. He was immediately sentenced to three years of reeducation through labor for "disturbing social order". After waiting to be released from prison, in 2000, Liu Xiaobo published three books: "The Nation Who Lies to the Conscience", "Selected Poems by Liu Xiaobo and Liu Xia", and "The Beauty Gives Me Mongolian Sweat Medicine" (coauthored with Wang Shuo). In 2008, Liu Xiaobo put forward the 6-point concept and 19-point proposal of Charter 08 on the 60th anniversary of the World Human Rights Day and the United Nations Universal Declaration of Human Rights, expounding the concepts of freedom, human rights, democracy, and constitutionalism, advocating for the revision of the constitution and the separation of power Checks and balances, the realization of legislative democracy, judicial independence, advocates freedom of association, assembly, speech, and religion. He was once again criminally detained on suspicion of inciting subversion of state power, and sentenced to 11 years in prison.

On October 8th of the same year, the Norwegian Nobel Committee awarded the 2010 Nobel Peace Prize on the grounds of "for his long and non-violent struggle for fundamental human rights in China" (for his long and non-violent struggle for fundamental human rights in China). Awarded to Liu Xiaobo. The Beijing authorities strongly protested and continued to imprison Liu Xiaobo. On the day of the award, the Nobel Peace Prize Committee represented Liu Xiaobo with an empty chair, and retained the certificate and bonus, waiting for Liu Xiaobo to receive it.

On May 31, 2017, Liu Xiaobo found abnormality during physical examination. On June 7, Liu Xiaobo was diagnosed with liver cancer by a doctor.

He was finally released from the prison where he was staying for 3103 days on "parole for medical treatment". On July 13, 2017, Liu Xiaobo died from multiple organ failure.

Sixty-one years of life, Liu Xiaobo once defend human rights with life, at some time in the past he was forced to bow to the system he protested against for the realistic environment, even used his tenacious vitality, compose one of the greatest chapters in the political history of modern China.

Tzemin Ition Tsai

# Now Available

Inner Child Press International

*presents*

W.A.R.

*We Are Revolution*

*Poets for Humanity*

# Preface

Yes I am excited and feel accomplished as we are on the last leg of our seventh year of publishing what I and many others deem to be a worthy enterprise, *The Year of the Poet.*

This year we have aligned our vision with that of Nober Peace Prize Recipients. We have title this year's theme. The Year of Peace! Hopefully thorugh our sharing each month, our poetry can have a profound effect on our global consciousness and the need for peace while educating ourselves and our readership about some of the individuals who have made history through their efforts to promulgate peace for all of humanity.. We are on our way to hitting yet another milestone. Needless to say, I am elated.

To reiterate, our initial vision was to just perform at this level for the year of 2014. Since that time we have had the blessed opportunity to include many other wonderful poets, word artists and storytellers in the Poetry Posse from lands, cultures and persuasions all over the world. We have featured hundreds of additional poets, thereby introducing their poetic offerings to our vast global audience.

In keeping with our effort and vision to expand the awareness of poets from all walks by making this offerings accessible, we at Inner Child Press International will continue to make every volume a FREE Download. The books are also available for purchase at the affordable cost of $7.00 per volume.

In the previous years, our monthly themes were Flowers, Birds, Gemstones, Trees and Past Cultures. This coming year we have elected to continue our focus of choosing what we consider a significant subject . . . PEACE! In each month's volume you will have the opportunity to not only read at least one poem themed by our Poetry Posse members about such celebrated Peace Ambassadors, but we have included a few words about each individual in our prologue. We hope you find the poetic offerings insightful as we use our poetic form to relay to you what we too have learned through our research in making our offering available to you, our readership.

In closing, we would like to thank you for being an integral part of our amazing journey.

Enjoy our amazing featured poets . . . they are amazing!

*Building Cultural Bridges of Understanding . . .*

Bless Up . . . From the home in our hearts to yours


*Bill*

The Poetry Posse
Inner Child Press Ineternational


PS

Do Not forget about the World Healing, World Peace Poetry effort.

Available here

www.worldhealingworldpeacepoetry.com

**For Free Downloads of Previous Issues of
The Year of the Poet**

www.innerchildpress.com/the-year-of-the-poet

# World Healing World Peace
## 2020

## Poets for Humanity
### Now Available

www.innerchildpress.com/world-healing-world-peace-poetry

www.worldhealingworldpeacepoetry.com

www.worldhealingworldpeacefoundation.org

# Liu Xiaobo
## 2010

Each month for the year of 2020, which we have deemed as *The Year of Peace*, we at Inner Child Press International will be celebrating through our poetry a few Nobel Peace Prize Recipients who have contributed greatly to humanity via their particular avocations. This month of Julu 2020 you will find select poems from each Poetry Posse member on this month's celebrants.

In 2010, The Nobel Peace Prize was awarded to Liu Xiaobo

**For more information about visit :**
www.nobelprize.org/prizes/peace/2010/xiaobo
https://en.wikipedia.org/wiki/Liu_Xiaobo
www.hrw.org/tag/liu-xiaobo

Liu Xiaobo
1955-2017

World Healing, World Peace Foundation
*human beings for humanity*

worldhealingworldpeacefoundation.org

*Poets . . .*
*sowing seeds in the*
*Conscious Garden of Life,*
*that those who have yet to come*
*may enjoy the Flowers.*

Poets, Writers . . . know that we are the enchanting magicians that nourishes the seeds of dreams and thoughts . . . it is our words that entice the hearts and minds of others to believe there is something grand about the possibilities that life has to offer and our words tease it forth into action . . . for you are the Poet, the Writer to whom the Gift of Words has been entrusted . . .

~ wsp

*poetry is . . .*

Poetry succeeds where instruction fails.

~ wsp

I Fly

because

... said the Dreamer to the world.

I Can

www.iamjustbrill.com

# Gail
# Weston
# Shazor

This is a creative promise ~ my pen will speak to and for the world. Enamored with letters and respectful of their power, I have been writing for most of my life. A mother, daughter, sister and grandmother I give what I have been given, greatfilledly.

Author of . . .

"An Overstanding of an Imperfect Love"
&
Notes from the Blue Roof

Lies My Grandfathers Told Me

available at Inner Child Press.

www.facebook.com/gailwestonshazor
www.innerchildpress.com/gail-weston-shazor
navypoet1@gmail.com

# Tanka

So why do we march?

Because we haven't been seen

Because we truly

Truly need Tiananmen

To change a world on fire

## Storm Warning

In the infinite madness
Of catching onto the unfamiliar
I breathe in the spaces
Between your breath
And taste my name
At the corner of your mouth
My day rights itself
And even the lightening
Flashing in the south
Cannot move me
Easier moments float in
Against the smoke
Blowing palm leaves
Colored verdant among
The darkening skyline
And i feel you listening
To the sound of changing hues
At the ending
Of the beginning
Of all things

# Ministrations
*Senryu in 5 parts*

Hold my hand in yours
There is never a wrong time
For it to be right

I welcome your touch
Especially after not
For so very long

It is in this time
Of many middling moments
That I look for you

And as you look too
It is still doing something
Let me ease your work

It's in the split place
Of calluses that create
A fearless new life

# Alicja Maria Kuberska

.

Alicja Maria Kuberska – awarded Polish poetess, novelist, journalist, editor. She was born in 1960, in Świebodzin, Poland. She now lives in Inowrocław, Poland.

In 2011 she published her first volume of poems entitled: "The Glass Reality". Her second volume "Analysis of Feelings", was published in 2012. The third collection "Moments" was published in English in 2014, both in Poland and in the USA. In 2014, she also published the novel - "Virtual roses" and volume of poems "On the border of dream". Next year her volume entitled "Girl in the Mirror" was published in the UK and "Love me" , " (Not )my poem" in the USA. In 2015 she also edited anthology entitled "The Other Side of the Screen".

In 2016 she edited two volumes: "Taste of Love" (USA), "Thief of Dreams" ( Poland) and international anthology entitled " Love is like Air" (USA). In 2017 she published volume entitled "View from the window" (Poland). She also edits series of anthologies entitled "Metaphor of Contemporary" (Poland)

Her poems have been published in numerous anthologies and magazines in Poland, the USA, the UK, Albania, Belgium, Chile, Spain, Israel, Canada, India, Italy, Uzbekistan, Czech Republic, South Korea and Australia. She was a featured poet of New Mirage Journal ( USA) in the summer of 2011.

Alicja Kuberska is a member of the Polish Writers Associations in Warsaw, Poland and IWA Bogdani, Albania. She is also a member of directors' board of Soflay Literature Foundation.

# Sentenced for the Crime of Speaking
*A poem dedicated to Liu Xiaobo*

The speeches made by a modest man,
A professor of literature and philosophy,
Can be dangerous as an enemy army.
"Shut him up," said the important politicians

The words woke up the sleeping people
And allowed them to see the dirty reality.
They could get out of the propaganda vapours.
"Shut him up," said the distinguished officials.

He dared to join protesting students
When the Tiananmen Square
Was red because of innocent blood.
"Shut him up," said the lawyers and judges.

The barbed wires of a labour camp.
Were not able to hold back the statements
About injustice and torn constitution.
 "Shut him up," said the prison guards.

Nobody and nothing stopped him.
The star of democracy illuminated his road.
One man – the recidivist fighting for the truth,
undermined the totalitarian system.

## Coat

I wear a body like a cloak,
Patience, humility, years.
It's that time - it tore and I darned the holes.

My coat shrinks and disappears
With passing days,
Until one day it scatters and
So it is with all the coats.

And me? And what about me?
Perhaps they will hatch from the coat cocoon
And I will turn into a cricket.
It's a difficult metamorphosis,
The most difficult in life.

This is the price of immortality
Without the gift of eternal youth

## The Rainbow

I look for the rainbow every day.
It does not matter that the day is
Gloomy, foggy, cheerless
And the sky is covered by
Heavy, stormy clouds.

The rainbow sleeps
In the drops of rain.
Warmed with sunshine,
It stretches on the sky like a bow
And blooms with six colors.

I blow away the worries
Together with grey fog

Jackie
Davis
Allen

Jackie Davis Allen, otherwise known as Jacqueline D. Allen or Jackie Allen, grew up in the Cumberland Mountains of Appalachia. As the next eldest daughter of a coal miner father and a stay at home mother, she was the first in her family to attend and graduate from college. Her siblings, in their own right, are accomplished, though she is the only one, to date, that has discovered the gift of writing.

Graduating from Radford University, with a Bachelors of Science degree in Early Education, she taught in both public and private schools. For over a decade she taught private art classes to children both in her home and at a local Art and Framing Shop where she also sold her original soft sculptured Victorian dolls and original christening gowns.

She resides in northern Virginia with her husband, taking much needed get-aways to their mountain home near the Blue Ridge Mountains, a place that evokes memories of days spent growing up in the Appalachian Mountains.

A lover of hats, she has worn many. Following marriage to her college sweetheart, and as wife, mother, grandmother, teacher, tutor, artist, writer, poet and crafter, she is a lover of art and antiques, surrounding herself, always, with books, seeking to learn more.

In 2015 she authored *Looking for Rainbows, Poetry, Prose and Art*, and in 2017, *Dark Side of the Moon*. Both books of mostly narrative poetry were published by Inner Child Press and were edited by hulya n. yilmaz.

in 2019, No Illusions.Through the Looking Glass, which was nominated to be considered for a Pulitzer Prize by the publisher and editor of InnerChild Press, ltd.

http://www.innerchildpress.com/jackie-davis-allen.php
jackiedavisallen.com

# Liu Xiaobo

Not so long ago, in 2010,
A Chinese citizen, Liu Xiaobo,
Political dissident, prisoner,
Was awarded, a prize:
The Nobel Peace Prize.

Punished for advocating
Political reforms.
Received four prison terms
For his actions and views.

Not so long ago, Liu Xiaobo
Fought against the one-way party
Ruled by the Communists
That he hoped to change.

In 2017, at the age of sixty one,
He died from liver cancer.
Still under control, guarded
By Chinese Communists.

## No Longer a Secret

In the confidential telling of his story
He desires that it be known,
World-round, that he has chosen to repent.
He confesses that it was he, who, today humbly prays
                  Pardon for the seeds of blame
                  And the shame that he has sown.

And, of the secrets he intentionally whispered.
Of those he inadvertently released, he pleads idleness
Of sensitivity, ashamed now of his immaturity.
And, of the umbrella, beneath which his sense
                  Of obscurity sought importance, he says
                  He misappropriated too much of self's delusion.

The white ghost of incrimination
Still comes round during the sleepless hours.
It circles still his bed chamber
Like an expanding storm of regret,
                  Beneath clouds of increasing gloom,
                  a dark storm prevails.

Beneath engaging eyes of indictment,
In need of forgiveness, rescue,
He throws off his contemptuous rags.
And humbly accepts God's mercy and grace.
                  Free at last, freed from that
                  Which once held him hostage.

# Good Morning

This morning I awakened
To skies gray and wet,
And as from the high heavens above
Streamed down, torrents of intent.

From my window seat, I spied
A small squirrel, dark and dank.
He was shivering and chattering;
Suddenly, he wisely scattered.

A bolt of destructive bright light
Startlingly burst into fury's flames
The clouds, revealing copious tears,
Released their pain, their angst.

No matter the name of the season,
No matter the time of day or of night,
Nature delights in revealing different
And surprising aspects of her face.

Once hidden from view, I now
Welcome anew, the face of the sun,
Bestowing ardent kisses in colors
Passionately.  Bravely, bright against blue.

Crossing high over the morning sky
I receive a gift, a needed reminder.
It is a rainbow  It is God's promise.
His covenant graciously renewed.

Tzemin

Ition

Tsai

Dr. Tzemin Ition Tsai (蔡澤民博士) was born in Republic of China, in 1957. He holds a Ph.D. in Chemical Engineering and two Masters of Science in Applied Mathematics and Chemical Engineering. He is a professor at Asia University (Taiwan), editor of "Reading, Writing and Teaching" academic text. He also writes the long-term columns for Chinese Language Monthly in Taiwan.

He is a scholar with a wide range of expertise, while maintaining a common and positive interest in science, engineering and literature member. He is also an editor of "Reading, Writing and Teaching" academic text and a columnist for *'Chinese Language Monthly'* in Taiwan

He has won many national literary awards. His literary works have been anthologized and published in books, journals, and newspapers in more than 40 countries and have been translated into more than a dozen languages.

# The Wailing of the Old System

When people say it's an old system
I should know
Overtones of the language
But I am not sure
What's better than me is waiting to replace me
What is better than me
An invisible and hollow musket
By what
You can blame me ruthlessly on my already ragged clothes

When people hid in the protected air-raid shelter
The eyes facing me
The pairs seem to be smiling
Don't know when
I became old and poor and useless
In addition
To picking up the seeds covered with sand on the ground
Waiting for spring to sprout
Before permission
I don't know when it will come gracefully

Far away, burning torches
Getting closer
Couldn't see the bright crossing my shadow
Tried to bend my knees
Find a proper vivid world on the soft ground
Close to the new buds of the young tender grass
Sharp aroma
No extra words
Straddle the shoulders to talk to me
I can only smile except turning my neck
Just like you did to me before

# Empty Chair, I Am In Your Words

Culture seem can be revolutionized
I can see it in you
Freedom seems not to be restricted
I heard in your words
Although the time to talk to you has passed
Those various opportunities
Will definitely reappear again

In your heart
Attempt to despise traditional culture
Your actions
Go back to the education program of following the
predecessor
No way to experience the value of your words
How to identify the inevitable reflection for a new aesthetic
trend
The crisis facing literature in the new era
Not so obvious and easy to see

Forgive my bluntness
This is not a struggle and pursuit of mockery
I am voluntarily called an alienated personality
And don't know how to start from self-denial
The Chinese literary world
Lacks characters with challenging attitudes
Chinese writers still
Lack personality awareness
I am the withered vitality attached to that impersonal deep
layer

Don't let rationality constrain emotional life
Don't let the empty chair continue to wait
Don't even
Yield, silence, or praise to tyranny
Don't testify to me
No army has ever killed anyone on Tiananmen Square

# Once Upon A Midnight Plain

To warn me about the tree
They are perfumed from unseen precis
It was wee
A slender little hut stands so lonely there
And so I screamed, 'Is that a tree diagram?'
The primitive age hesitates in the mud of lost
I uncovered the savanna
My mind always strays to herbivores
Remembering many beetle, narrative pollinators
The stemmed silver tree sapping
The lupine lowland landscaping
I crave the auld, arborical attractiveness
And the leafy spurge never recapping
I had dreamed of sedges unwrapping
Only this and a peach
What could there be more purely dreich?
There stood a puckery long beach
Night brings beauty
The peach smiled
It was fluty, mild, profiled!
The handsome honey harvesting
The citrus coati cornering
Beading and beading with my pear
In there, stepped a caraway narrative

Tzemin Ition Tsai

# Shareef Abdur Rasheed

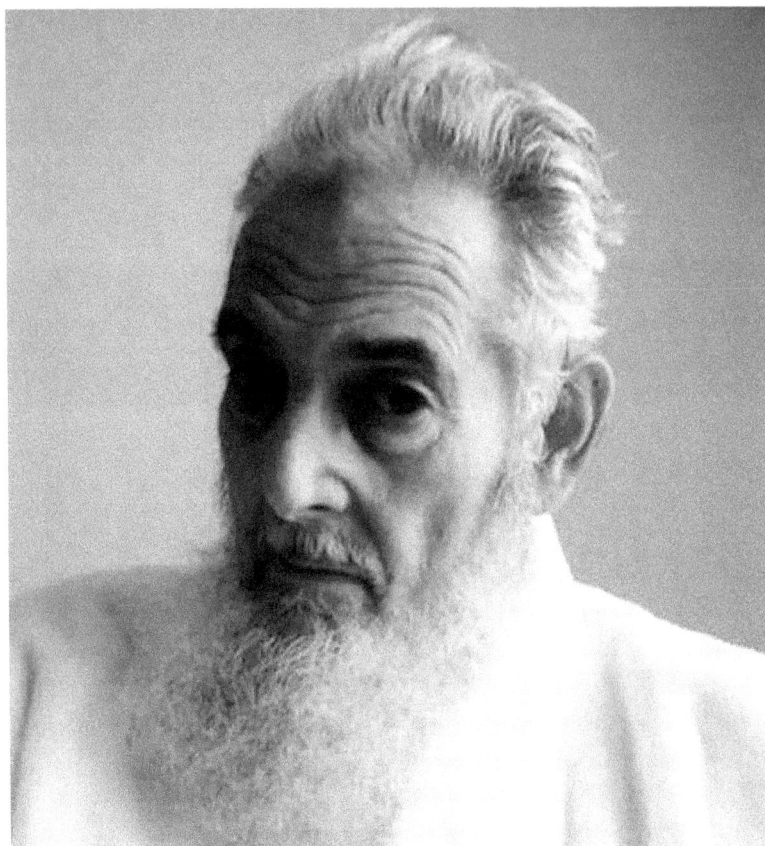

Shareef Abdur-Rasheed, AKA Zakir Flo was born and raised in Brooklyn, New York. His education includes Brooklyn College, Suffolk County Community College and Makkah, Saudi Arabia. He is a Veteran of the Viet Nam era, where in 1969 he reverted to his now reverently embraced Islamic Faith. He is very active in the Islamic community and beyond with his teachings, activism and his humanity.

Shareef's spiritual expression comes through the persona of "Zakir Flo" . Zakir is Arabic for "To remind". Never silent, Shareef Abdur-Rasheed is always dropping science, love, consciousness and signs of the time in rhyme.

Shareef is the Patriarch of the Abdur-Rasheed Family with 9 Children (6 Sons and 3 Daughters) and 41 Grandchildren (24 Boys and 17 Girls).

For more information about Shareef, visit his personal FaceBook Page at :

https://www.facebook.com/shareef.abdurrasheed1
https://zakirflo.wordpress.com

# enigma

----------

wrapped in a contradiction
liu Xiaobo bravery in Chinese
mainland unquestioned
standing against brutal force
rose up against the odds
insane odds to question
a system without any tolerance
for dissent, descend upon
status quo of a nation
that prided itself in mass
intense domination of it's
people totally
occupy the very souls
of the masses
rendering them submissive
an understatement
Liu railed against the machine
thus banished from the everyday
functions that constitute freedom,
what freedom?
imprisoned in a prison
that resides in a prison
for his efforts got the prize
but overall, he's being regarded,
rewarded perplexing
considering he backed oppression
of American imperialism
invading Muslim lands
engaging in crimes against humanity
supported Zionist Israel in their
oppression, genocide of
Palestinian peoples

therefore, selective activism against
Chinese oppression but in total
agreement to sustained imperialism
translating into crimes against humanity
an odd nod of approval to
a strange gravitation
gave him the prize anyway
hooray, hooray
so, what does that say for
substance or legitimacy?


food4thought = education

## please stay close to me
--------------------

your majesty he who
monopolized legitimacy
over all other would be kings
they have no supremacy,
them who come, go fade away
all fake comparatively
their death inevitably
hangs over head constantly
they were not given immortality
their stay is temporary
they were made that way
by he who fashioned universe,
ocean, sky, mountains, seas,
you and me and all creation
just by proclaiming " BE " and it was,
and it is and it will be
he who has no beginning,
no end was not begotten nor does
he begets
he (Allah) is one (1) he is eternal,
there is nothing that compares
in a class by himself period.

he is not creation he is the creator
him alone worthy of worship
far removed from taqhut (false deities)
the likes of which is attributed to thee
by folk misguided
those who take truth and hide it
instead take fake
try to disguise it until that day
comes their way and all souls

will realize that truth
prevails over falsehood
can not be watered down
to appease men's needs
fulfill their greed, bring ease
to the fact they don't believe,
didn't heed

far removed is he from all needs
not like his creation
who has limitations?
creator does not need creation
creation needs creator

do not worship any creation
nor their false gods,
imitations all fake!!
lands, nations, tribes,
cultures created by man
including their flags
are not sacred, holy
nor do they deserve
praise, devotion, glory
they are all things of man
only creator deserves,
praise, glory, worship,
devotion, submission

mankind's tribal cultures,
traditions
designed to deter one from
giving all praise, glory, worship,
devotion, submission
to only Allah*(swt) exclusively
the only purpose for which he

created thee
thus, hindering mankind
from the straight path
that on which creator bestowed
his eternal grace
not of them who went astray
ultimately receive eternal
damning disgrace

*(swt) = all glory to Allah.


food4thought = education

## mind fields..,
--------------

life blood drains into ageless sands
without so much as a whimper
those in the vicinity are too caught up
with dismal prospects projecting
dismal outcome expected
or better yet symbols
representing better days
when life seemed simple
though one may ask " when was life
ever simple?
is it even in its DNA?
based on what we live through everyday
what's simple anyway?
the way days play through life's acts
from when the curtain went up on act one
where the fair maiden soaking in the sun
was set upon by men with guns
who wanted some?
that get attention in the name of tension
generated, love it or hate it
folk come ' n ' go through the generations
going through energetic gyrations
flowing with the cosmos blow
yes or no come on ya'll know
that just ain't so
never the less they still come ' n ' go
and do we ever ask questions,
so, take time to know
what direction life flows
cradle to grave we're slaves
either to the lord or the crave
" Don't make your flesh your lord "

say'eth lord of lords, king of kings
"constantly turn to me, remember me
so, your soul may have eyes that see
and your ears hear the songbird sing


food4thought = education

# Kimberly Burnham

A brain health expert with a PhD in Integrative Medicine, Kimberly Burnham has lived in tropical Colombia; in Belgium during the Vietnam War; in Japan teaching businessmen English; in diverse international Toronto, Canada and several places in the US. Now, she's in Spokane, WA with her wife, Elizabeth, two sets of twins (age 11 & 14) and three dogs. Her recent book, *Awakenings: Peace Dictionary, Language and the Mind, a Daily Brain Health Program* includes the word for peace in hundreds of languages. Kim's poetry weaves through 70 volumes of *The Year of the Poet, Inspired by Gandhi, Women Building the World, A Woman's Place in the Dictionary*, Tiferet Journal, Human/Kind Journal and more.

https://www.nervewhisperer.solutions/
https://www.linkedin.com/in/kimberlyburnham/

## Peaceful Neighborhood

Who doesn't want a peaceful neighborhood?

the Japanese where peace is "heiwa" do

Singaporeans ranked seventh in a world of peaceful

nations use the same characters 平和

pronounced "peng ann" or "hépíng" in Chinese

while the Korean Kim Dae-jung worked

for "p'yŏnghwa" and human rights

winning a Nobel Peace Prize in 2000

what have we learned and done even more

in the last twenty years

# Life in A Pair of Characters

Many Korean words
written with a pair of characters

like peace "pyeonghwa" 평화

the first character also
first of fair and equality
as if without fairness there is no peace
and the first of reputation, calmness, average
we can be calm with an average reputation
also appraisal and review with weekday
and oddly breaststroke

but note that 평평 means flat

like a flat playing field on which everyone
has enough food, shelter and peace


The second character of peace
same for harmony, ignition and digestion
and all the rest have commonality with peace
telephone, culture, conversation
a peaceful conversation about culture on the telephone
mural, deterioration, reinforcement
myth and comic all end
in the same character as peace

# Peace Around the World in Fibonacci Syllables

1. Paz,
1. Paix,
2. Shanti,
3. Fred, Cánti,
5. P'yŏnghwa, Zhi bde, Kuc
8. Friede Diim-deih-naa:k, Kötöhati,
13. all kinds of words for peace don't mean
the same thing to all
21. they mean calm, slow, quiet, satisfied, level, tame,
still, comfort, soft liver, not war and
34. gentle, good character, cold, legible, words of peace
spiral through the world of Salaam, Moyo-dame, Ɖutifafa,
Wóda khota, Hɛra, Vrede
21. Kérta, Damai, Nuisar of, Têntrême, Rabula, Jingsuk,
Pêameyış, ʔčhuâyk kyō čI,
13. Angkan pengker nintimratin, Údo, Amahoro
8. Anachemowegan, Мир, Hépíng,
5. Tancos, Yatanpa
3. Aman, Ta,
2. Nyens nyens,
1. Pé,
1. Dör.

# Elizabeth E. Castillo

Elizabeth Esguerra Castillo is a multi-awarded and an Internationally-Published Contemporary Author/Poet and a Professional Writer / Creative Writer / Feature Writer / Journalist / Travel Writer from the Philippines. She has 2 published books, "Seasons of Emotions" (UK) and "Inner Reflections of the Muse", (USA). Elizabeth is also a co-author to more than 60 international anthologies in the USA, Canada, UK, Romania, India. She is a Contributing Editor of Inner Child Magazine, USA and an Advisory Board Member of Reflection Magazine, an international literary magazine. She is a member of the American Authors Association (AAA) and PEN International.

## Web links:

Facebook Fan Page

https://free.facebook.com/ElizabethEsguerraCastillo

Google Plus

https://plus.google.com/u/0/+ElizabethCastillo

# Light and Darkness

A man born to fight for freedom,

Standing up against tyranny

A champion of freedom of expression

The light amidst the darkness,

Xiaobo once said, "I have no enemies."

For if there is no hatred

All will live in unity

Xiaobo-the Light who illuminated the path

Fought to gain peace and harmony.

# Undefined Love

Dawn is about to set
Here I am still thinking of you
Your shadow vanishing in the moonlit night,
I walked the dark path to realize you're not there
Were you just an illusion, a dream, or were created by just
pure imagination
All I know is that you possess those pair of eyes that
glimmer in the dark
That even if I get lost anywhere in this world, I may find
myself again in you,
You're more than the word Love itself for I cannot simply
define how you swept me off my feet
A meager stare from you sets my heart in so much
commotion
And hearing you call my name in such an intricate way sets
my soul on fire,
Find me again, take my hand and let's go to the end of the
world
There at the tower let us watch the moon while some
clouds dance in the background
As the splashing of waves make sounds while we walk by
the shoreline barefooted,
Feeling the warm sand beneath our feet with a mild breeze
brushing our cheeks
Find me again in another lifetime where we could define
this eternal love we share transcending time and space.

# The Fault in Our Stars

You made me see the Universe in a different way,
We created our little infinity
In such a short time
We had our forever
And after you're gone,
I'll never be the same again.
'Coz the magic vanished in an instant
But the beautiful fragments of memories will linger
For in every song that I hear
In every literature that I read,
In every sunset and moonlit night I witness,
Will always remind me of you.
You and me-
We are lost stars
Star-crossed lovers beyond time
Sharing beautiful coincidences.
I am your Moon
And you are my brightest star
In another lifetime
We will see each other again
To continue our story
By then you and I
Will be reunited by our own flames
For our little infinity has no end.

# Joe
# Paire

# Joe Paire

Joseph L Paire' aka Joe DaVerbal Minddancer . . .
is a quiet man, born in a time where civil liberties
were a walk on thin ice. He's been a victim of his
own shyness often sidelined in his own quest for
love. He became the observer, charting life's path.
Taking note of the why, people do what they do. His
writings oft times strike a cord with the
dormant strings of the reader. His pen the rosined
bow drawn across the mind. He comes full-frontal
or in the subtlest way, always expressing in a way
that stimulate the senses.

www.facebook.com/joe.minddancer

# Behind These Walls

The teaching, the preaching, the beatings
The meditation of maybe I can save them
I'm lonely better not speak out but how can I be silent
Life tastes sweet in increments
How can I not understand oppressions of expression?
Leaders teach by experienced examples
The lead now follows in the mindset of us.
Gee if I could conjure up perfect philosophies
This is no democracy just sticks on top of me
Dictator's dictate the law to me
Don't talk about Me, or the country
Men! Countrymen, wanted men, hunted man
Sorted and deported some never seen again

A gained freedom,
never equals an earned freedom to men
welcome to the jungle, Liu Xiaobo
noble prize for a noble life
we all wish we had that normal life
it never mattered if you wore it
warriors' never fight for the medal
one's personal metal can do so much
you're silent on this plain
the ultimate understanding of fellow
does the bellows still blow?
Born 12/28/1955, flew 7/13/2017
2020 Noble Peace Prize winner
Liu Xiaobo died in jail, Love the worlds people.

# Rainy Daze

I've walked this path before
It's not familiar to me now
Have I emerged from a sleep still dreaming?

Cancer has a funny way to remind me
Of what's behind my steps
People see the 20-20 scene
There are ashes everywhere

Feckless in a land I once knew
There's nothing left to save
There are no more rights
Listless as I listen to dead birds

Wake-up was a call heard in slumber
I can't answer honestly if I'm not
I was not in reverse years
Am I free now for I have not seen a soul?

I've run away before
Never escaping the choice before me
Have I emerged from a dream still asleep?

## Party Boys

I saw love today
Minding my business as usual
Nature took its time
and timed the fall of a leaf on my shoulder

listen to the rays' hand cupping bare limbs
has winter come to claim its spoils?
neath that leaf lay larvae
no harm shall befall the innocent

I was King for a moment
Is this how love truly works?
I felt something inside although I hide my empathy
Its okay to feel although I battle with pride
I who refuse to cry shout, set them free

I raked the remaining leaves, piled high and purposeful
Flags and symbols of wretched memories
Fenced in to be absorbed into the earth
Dispersed in the universe where love was found

I saw love today
My business is no longer proving who I am
Nature doesn't take time with the human mind
We are all family neath our leaves
Which way will the wind blow?

# hülya

# n.

# yılmaz

Liberal Arts Emerita, hülya n. yılmaz is a published author, literary translator, and Co-Chair and Director of Editing Services at Inner Child Press International. Her poetic work appeared in an excess of eighty-five anthologies of global endeavors and has been presented at numerous national and international poetry events. In 2018, the Writer's International Network of British Colombia, Canada honored yılmaz with a literary award. As of 2017, two of her poems remain permanently installed in *Telepoem Booth* – a U.S.-wide poetic art exhibition. hülya finds it vital for everyone to understand a deeper sense of self, and writes creatively to attain a comprehensive awareness for and development of our humanity.

Writing Web Site
https://hulyanyilmaz.com/

Editing Web Site
https://hulyasfreelancing.com

## uninspired

our birth dates are identical
he met death in 2017; my turn: unknown as of yet
a student of literature and philosophy,
a literary critic, and a university lecturer . . .
i should feel connected beyond a search engine,
as our past experiences have been the same
what, though, have i discovered in him
that which can reach beneath the mere surface?

not much
nothing that would be original, that is
pieces of generic information galore
i, however, always quest to learn more,
much more

i have tried and tried again
only to realize that my efforts were in vain

for a frustratingly long enough time,
before my computer i sat idly
showing off my fingerprints,
the screen looked back at me
if only this gadget could talk,
what would it utter, i wondered

you have my sincere apologies, Dr. Xiaobo
for being this uninspired today
in case someone might read these few words of mine
here are a few facts about you, found easily online

the courage with which you armed yourself in 1989
to protest alongside 100,000 students in Tiananmen Square

for democracy, free speech, and a free press
is your gift not only to China or the Chinese
but to each citizen of the world,
to humanity in its entirety
you have endured five years of debilitating chains
three, in prison; two, in labour camps

"sentenced for the crime of speaking"

you resisted
you persisted

you kept fighting for democracy,
dedicating over twenty years of your life
to your demands for the constitutional rights
of your nation as spelled out in Article 35 . . .
"freedom of speech, of the press, of assembly,
of association, of procession and of demonstration"

powers that be also resisted, persisted
you still dared to co-write Charta 08 in 2008
and advocated for your country's shift toward democracy

in the month of December in the year of 2009
the assembly of the utterly corrupted jailed you again
the chains stayed with you for eleven years this time around

"sentenced for undermining the state authorities"

in your justified denying of the charges,
you have maintained your landmark assertion:
"Opposition is not the same as undermining."

then came the year of 2010
the Nobel Peace Prize Committee found you . . .

# Silencing the Conscience

"Did you see that?"

*I most certainly did.*

"Let's go. We must help."

*What for?*

"For justice!"

*I cannot fix each wrong.*

"We must start somewhere!"

*Sit down! This isn't about you. MOB!*


What IF . . .

it is about you one day?

# A Renga for Liu Xiaobo

*My dear poet-friends:*

*Your collaboration is needed on this one.*

*Here is my stanza . . .*


Tiananmen and students

Constitutional

Red Massacre

hülya n. yılmaz

# Teresa E. Gallion

Teresa E. Gallion

Teresa E. Gallion was born in Shreveport, Louisiana and moved to Illinois at the age of 15. She completed her undergraduate training at the University of Illinois Chicago and received her master's degree in Psychology from Bowling Green State University in Ohio. She retired from New Mexico state government in 2012.

She moved to New Mexico in 1987. While writing sporadically for many years, in 1998 she started reading her work in the local Albuquerque poetry community. She has been a featured reader at local coffee houses, bookstores, art galleries, museums, libraries, Outpost Performance Space, the Route 66 Festival in 2001 and the State of Oklahoma's Poetry Festival in Cheyenne, Oklahoma in 2004. She occasionally hosts an open mic.

Teresa's work is published in numerous Journals and anthologies. She has two CDs: *On the Wings of the Wind* and *Poems from Chasing Light*. She has published three books: *Walking Sacred Ground, Contemplation in the High Desert* and *Chasing Light.*

*Chasing Light* was a finalist in the 2013 New Mexico/Arizona Book Awards.

The surreal high desert landscape and her personal spiritual journey influence the writing of this Albuquerque poet. When she is not writing, she is committed to hiking the enchanted landscapes of New Mexico. You may preview her work at

*http://bit.ly/1aIVPNq* or *http://bit.ly/13IMLGh*

# Liu Xiaobo Legacy of Non-Violence

Liu Xiaobo supported the people of China
through his non-violent resistance
against the oppression of the Communist Party.

In addition to being a human rights activist, he
was a philosopher, writer and literary critic.
Throughout life he experienced literary fame,
persisted in non-violent resistance and spent
quite a few years in prison.

He was awarded the Nobel Peace Prize
in 2010 while in prison for his non-violent
struggle for basic human rights in China.
The government denied him the honor
of receiving the prize.

# Map of Love

Your body is a map of love
that transcends boundaries.
I cruise on your landscape
in awe of the love that enfolds me.

I am seeking the right coordinates
to hug and run wild within
the fertile trails binding your love.

Each move I make brings me
closer to your essence
for your boundaries are sacred.
Holiness marks the regions
of your map.

My plea without words
tremble with a humble request.
May I stay here with you forever?

# Heaven's Window

She looked out the window
watching me walk the light path.
The smile on her face radiated
a love only a sister can give.

I saw a distant window felt
my sister's presence waiting.
The path became brighter
as I struggled to continue.
My journey was long and rough.

I bathed in fear, anger, pride,
lust and greed.  Survived
the bloodletting at every turn.
Determination was my wrist band.

My spiritual guide always walked
a safe distance behind me
to pick me up in case I fell.

My sister's chest was threatening
to explode.  But she knew,
she could not move.

I had to walk that last mile alone
to reach her embrace.

# Ashok K. Bhargava

Ashok Bhargava is a poet, writer, community activist, public speaker, management consultant and a keen photographer. Based in Vancouver, he has published several collections of his poems: Riding the Tide, Mirror of Dreams, A Kernel of Truth, Skipping Stones, Half Open Door and Lost in the Morning Calm. His poetry has been published in various literary magazines and anthologies.

Ashok is a Poet Laureate and poet ambassador to Japan, Korea and India. He is founder of WIN: Writers International Network Canada. Its main objective is to inspire, encourage, promote and recognize writers of diverse genres, artists and community leaders. He has received many accolades including Nehru Humanitarian Award for his leadership of Writers International Network Canada, Poets without Borders Peace Award for his journeys across the globe to celebrate peace and to create alliances with poets, and Kalidasa Award for creative writings.

# A Way of Seeing …

*this poem is dedicated to Liu Xiaobo*

no force can
put an end
to human quest for justice

soldiers ruthlessly
trample on peaceful marchers
with gas and pepper spray

it's like people don't matter
no rights
no freedoms

protestors keep pouring in -
seeds birthing
more seeds

they chant
we have no enemy
we have no hatred

## With You

I am transformed
I feel
a brand-new world
unfolds for me

I smile with joy and
discover how selfless
love exists
in you

I discover
a fascinating full moon
and an amazing morning sun
inside me

I ask myself
how so much joy can spring
from everything
so ordinary

Maybe it is ME
who has grown ordinary
Maybe . . . over long, long years
I just grew smaller

## Time-Lapse

You said it so casually –
let's just be strangers from now on
as if we had no past.

Without waiting
you hide your face
and turn away.

For months we were together
like a tree and a vine
entwined

breathing in the same space
but now I am a tree
seeing you flow away

like a river.

Caroline
'Ceri Naz'
Nazareno
Gabis

# Carolin 'Ceri' Nazareno-Gabis

Caroline 'Ceri Naz' Nazareno-Gabis, World Poetry Canada International Director to Philippines is known as a 'poet of peace and friendship', a multi-awarded poet, editor, journalist, speaker, linguist, educator, peace and women's advocate. She believes that learning other's language and culture is a doorway to wisdom.

Among her poetic belts include 7 th Prize Winner in the 19 th and 20 th Italian Award of Literary Festival; Writers International Network-Canada ''Amazing Poet 2015'', The Frang Bardhi Literary Prize 2014 (Albania), the sair-gazeteci or Poet Journalist Award 2014 (Tuzla, Istanbul, Turkey) and World Poetry Empowered Poet 2013 (Vancouver, Canada). She's a featured member of Association of Women's Rights and Development (AWID), The Poetry Posse, Galaktika Poetike, Asia Pacific Writers and Translators (APWT ), Axlepino and Anacbanua.

Her poetry and children's stories have been featured in different anthologies and magazines worldwide.

Links to her works:

panitikan.ph/2018/03/30/caroline-nazareno-gabis
apwriters.org/author/ceri_naz
www.aveviajera.org/nacionesunidasdelasletras/id1181
.html

# No Enemies, No Hatred

The Man Called Liu Xiaobo
Created a universe of love,
No time for hatred,
Time has been conditioned
To love and be loved,

His regime dispelled  hate for love
everywhere-equal
infinite and eminent
within-and-beyond reality
experiences shape  perceptions
which in turn guides our actions...

Liu, you are the voice of the humanity!

## in between

your eyes are lights
thy lips unsealed
while kissing the sparks
of serenity
in the eve
and predawn
of your own

until everything
solely connects
deep down
yourself
within.

## Orenda

Mystical garden
In Gaia's face
Ceaseless energy
Intangible waves
 of awakened soul,

when the dawn whispers
serenity in my ears,
I am synergy,
When the prayer
Keeps on humming
Contemplation in reverie,
I am satisfaction
When my feet touch
The delightful earth.

Swapna
Behera

Swapna Behera is a bilingual contemporary poet, author, translator and editor from Odisha, India. She was a teacher from 1984 to 2015. Her stories, poems and articles are widely published in National and International journals, and ezines, and are translated into different national and International languages. She has penned six books. She is the recipient of the Prestigious International Mother Language UGADI AWARD WINNER 2019. She was conferred upon the Prestigious International Poesis Award of Honor at the 2nd Bharat Award for Literature as Jury in 2015, The Enchanting Muse Award in India World Poetree Festival 2017, World Icon of Peace Award in 2017, and the Pentasi B World Fellow Poet in 2017. She is the recipient of Gold Cross of Wisdom Award, the Prolific Poetess Award, The Life time Achievement Award, The Best Planner Award, The Sahitya Shiromani Award, ATAL BIHARI BAJPAYEE AWARD 2018, Ambassador De Literature Award 2018, Global Literature Guardian Award, International Life Time Achievement Award and the Master of Creative Impulse Award. She has received the Honoured Poet of India from the Seychelles Government accredited Literary Society LLSF. Her one poem A NIGHT IN THE REFUGEE CAMP is translated into 50 languages. She is the Ambassador of Humanity by Hafrikan Prince Art World Africa 2018 and an official member of World Nation's Writers Union, Kazakhstan 2018. Italy, the National President for India by Hispanomundial Union of Writers (UHE), Peru, the administrator of several poetic groups, and the Cultural Ambassador for India and south Asia of Inner Child Press U.S.

# slogans of a dark horse

history codes ....
long non-violent struggle
for fundamental rights in China
eleven years of imprisonment
two years of deprivation of political rights
the first Chinese scholar to win the Nobel peace prize
that to an empty chair represented him
for he was in the prison or detention
a poet, essayist, critic, activist and thinker
author of "No enemies; No hatred"
his slogan
freedom of expression is
the foundation of human rights
the source of humanity and the mother of truth
life is priceless even to an ant
if you want to go to hell don't complain of the dark
patriotism is a villain's last refuge
hatred is corrosive of wisdom
he was called
a dark horse for his radical opinions
for he criticised the Chinese tradition
of Confucianism
author of "going naked towards God''
"the fog of metaphysics"
a professor of Jilin University
son of a nursery teacher
a human right activist
he is professor Liu Xiaobo
history remembers ....

# don't ever call me from the back

I am on my sojourn journey
if I turn and show my mask less face
you can only see my pure nudity
isn't nudity a bliss?
sky is nude;
a hill is nude
a new born is nude;
a dew drop is nude
a soul is nude
without gender and colour
blessed are those who sing the psalm with humility
there is always a joy to listen the stream
 the care taker of this bone cage is in hibernation
eyes are caves of Adam
heaven is a document of fools
nights are customised manuscripts
 a man stammers in lust and love
 since long I have never seen the carnival of love
 love is a drop of water for a crow
who doesn't carry pebbles to throw in the pot?
but I am a scare crow
guarding my inner self
my ego and super ego
I am a cadaver on the road march
obviously, I don't have a heart
so also, a drop of blood ...
as I am a dead God ....

# and a thousand times

and a thousand times
I search the bald island
where I can sow verses
monsoon clouds will sing Nirvana
the seed will die anonymously
to inscribe the colours of twinkling stars
the domain of poetry will glow
from every terrace in the form of a radiant smiles
"here it is ........."
whispers the grass...
twits the bird within......

# Albert 'Infinite' Carrasco

Albert "Infinite The Poet" Carrasco is an urban poet, mentor and public speaker.

Albert believes his experience of growing up in poverty, dealing with drugs and witnessing murder over and over were lessons learnt, in order to gain knowledge to teach. Albert's harsh reality and honesty is a powerfully packed punch delivered through rhyme. Infinite grew up in the east part of the Bronx and still resides there, so he knows many young men will follow the same dark path he followed looking for change. The life of crime should never be an option to being poor but it is, very often.

Infinite poetry @lulu.com

Alcarrasco2 on YouTube

Infinite the poet on reverbnation

## Infinite Poetry

http://www.lulu.com/us/en/shop/al-infinite-carrasco/infinite-poetry/paperback/product-21040240.html

# Liu Xiaobo

Liu Xiaobo was born in Changchun China to a family of intellectuals.
His contributions to the world as a human rights activist made china's future brighter.
He was a very educated man,
a philosopher.
Liu Xiaobo Was a laureate of literary art,
In jilin university he founded a poetry group called "the innocent hearts.
He would receive his bachelor's and PhD and become a lecturer.
Because of Liu Xiaobos views he was given the label of the "dark horse"
But no matter what he wouldn't stray away from thoughts and maintained a steady course.
He was incarcerated for his protest and false claims of inciting riots,
In order to make change to the communist one party rule, there was no way for him to remain quiet.
In 2010 Liu Xiaobo was awarded the Nobel peace prize for his non violent struggle for
Human rights in China, it was fundamental.

## She got away

She was supposed to be mine. We met as youngens, young teens running these BX streets buggn. When she met me I was already floss'n, block hugg'n and gat buss'n, but I don't think she knew how I was really hold'n. I was feel'n shorty, the don was gonna put her on and make sure she didn't live another day in poverty. She could've been my ride and die, but when I rode out i always saw her with guys. I wouldn't catch feelings, I understood the game, I gave her ample time to be mine and down the line bear my name. We both was moving fast, me in the streets on the ave, her under sheets bounc'n her ass, I couldn't complain, it is what it is so I stood in my lane. I knew all the hustlers in Hell's Kitchen, dudes talk so I knew all the randoms she was hitt'n... ayo Inf you know so and so, she's a freak we did this that and a third, basic nikkas are treat'n her like a bird. Yeah I know her, I'm not going to deny it, that's my homie, is how I responded, She was using what she had, to get what she wanted. I always wondered about what could've been, because i played my "friend" position and stood in the cut like  Excoriation. Through the years we didn't talk much, we lost touch, she slipped...my clutch.

# Homage to the OG's

Spanish OG's loved me, they knew I was the future king in the projects to rep Puerto Rico in the arena of Manteca and perico. The name was ringing bells and paper was long, respect was massive and the team was strong. Vayas con dios is something they always told me, they didn't actually want me to go with god, they was referring to his guidance as i was caught up in a life prone to violence. They didn't throw me in the fire, I was raised on the surface of hell, they just knew life would be better for them when I rose to power. I was coming up learning the ropes, they stopped stick up kids from robbing me, then they scolded me, Bellaco you're off point, you gotta tote, gotta be on point for these robberies and those tryn to cut throat. They told me about everything from A-Z, I listened to what they told me, knowledge was gained, a few of them got to see the come up, a lot of them died preaching the game. They held me down so I reciprocated the favor, I made them untouchable, the walked around with Kangols,Guayaberas, pinky rings and 24 karat Cubans and gold teeth clear of any danger, if violated the BX quickly turned to the old San Juan's La Perla.

# Eliza Segiet

Eliza Segiet: Master's Degree in Philosophy, completed postgraduate studies in Cultural Knowledge, Philosophy, Arts and Literature at Jagiellonian University. She is a member of The Association of Polish Writers and The NWNU - Union of Writers of the World.

Her poems *Questions* and *Sea of Mists* won the title of the International Publication of the Year 2017 and 2018 in Spillwords Press.

For her volume of *Magnetic People,* she won a literary award of a *Golden Rose* named after Jaroslaw Zielinski (Poland 2019 r.). Her poem The *Sea of Mists* was chosen as one of the best one hundred poems of 2018 by International Poetry Press Publication Canada.

In Poet's Yearbook, as the author of *Sea of Mists*, she was awarded with the prestigious Elite Writer's Status Award as one of the best poets of 2019 (July 2019).

She was awarded *World Poetic Star Award* by World Nations Writers Union – the world's largest Writers' Union from Kazakhstan (August 2019).

In September 2019 she was 1st Place Laureate (Foreign Poetry category) – in Contest *Quando È la Vita ad Invitare* for poem *Be Yourself* (Italy).

Her poem *Order* from volume *Unpaired* was selected as one of the 100 best poems of 2019 in International Poetry Press Publications (Canada).

Nominated for the Pushcart Prize 2019.

Nominated for the iWoman Global Awards (2019).

Laureate Naji Naaman Literary Prize 2020.

Laureate International Award PARAGON OF HOPE (Canada, 2020).

Obtained certificate of appreciation from *Gujarat Sahitya Academy* and *Motivational Strips* for literary excellence par with global standards (2020).

Ambassador of Literature granted by *Motivational Strips*.

Author's works can be found in anthologies, separate books and literary magazines worldwide.

## Asphyxiation
*In memory of Liu Xiaobo Nobel Peace Prize laureate in 2010*

In closure and in freedom
 - faithful to his convictions,
cause he knew,
that the right of every human being
should be the freedom of speech.
Without it
laws will be trampled,
and truth suppressed
won't grant a breath
to expression of thoughts

- it will stifle the humankind.

*Translated by Ula de B*

# Word

I cling to a reality
a quiet, peaceful
one, without hatred.

I am not interested in
language, origin, appearance.

I cling to a reality
in which the word freedom
is the same
as its meaning.


*Translated by Artur Komoter*

# Defense

She stopped being painless.
New times have taught her words that hurt,
acts
that do not allow
for unpunished human exploitation.

She does not only defend herself.
She does not allow for defamation,
she copes with reality
like others.

She is not soundless.

Sometimes she will shout something,
cry.

She is not colorless
even when she is silent
– with her eyes she can say

*no.*

*Translated by Artur Komoter*

# William S. Peters Sr.

Bill's writing career spans a period of over 50 years. Being first Published in 1972, Bill has since went on to Author in excess of 50 additional Volumes of Poetry, Short Stories, etc., expressing his thoughts on matters of the Heart, Spirit, Consciousness and Humanity. His primary focus is that of Love, Peace and Understanding!

Bill says . . .

I have always likened Life to that of a Garden. So, for me, Life is simply about the Seeds we Sow and Nourish. All things we "Think and Do", will "Be" Cause and eventually manifest itself to being an "Effect" within our own personal "Existences" and "Experiences" . . . whether it be Fruit, Flowers, Weeds or Barren Landscapes! Bill highly regards the Fruits of his Labor and wishes that everyone would thus go on to plant "Lovely" Seeds on "Good Ground" in their own Gardens of Life!

to connect with Bill, he is all things Inner Child

www.iaminnerchild.com

Personal Web Site

www.iamjustbill.com

## Against the odds
*Dedicated to the spirit of Liu Xiaobo*

I have pushed against the rivers
And attempted to change the flow . . .
For the people

I have attempted to capture the winds
That I may blow away the suffering
That the people have endured

I have painted the hammer
And the boot,
of subterfuge and oppression
in what I thought to be
invisible colors

yes, like you,
like us all,
I have dreamed of better days,
And regardless of their likeliness
To manifest,
I still
Pushed against the rivers,
Attempted to capture the winds,
And painted the hammer and the boot
In colors
I thought to be invisible . . .
Because I refused to believe
That I could not stand up
Against the odds

# Abducted

Rhetoric, rote, rites and propaganda,
Interlaced with lies and deceits
Misdirection and misgivings
With threads of far-reaching truths
Woven into the fabric
That the misrepresentation of truth
Can be upheld by argument

Minds molded
With emboldened statements
From the realms of 'looney land'
And beyond, and be-yonder
Stealing from the children
Their innate wonder . . .
Not a blunder,
But a plan

Man has always sought to control
The race, the game,
And any other challenge
That he may come to master
The outcome . . .
With the exception being him self !

Be it Religion, Politics or any other
Cultural identity,
They all have the same goal
Obeisance, Obedience
And Control
Over whomever
Is willing to listen
And those who do not as well

Time eventually
Will tell us
Where 'Truth'
Can be found, but not until
We attempt to
Ground ourselves
And reconnect
To our natural being

As I said,
Our children
Are being abducted
Every damn day . . .
Minds stolen,
Spirits suppressed
And wonder vilified
Leaving them in an
Emotional void,
Annoyed,
Devoid
Of any meaningful substance
That furthers the manifestation
And evolution
Of humanity
Towards its ideological goal

Some souls sold,
But most are just abducted
Into the realm
Of subtle and malleable truths

## embracing the sublime . . .

before me stood a Mountain
i knew i had to climb
for the Valleys that were in my life
have passed beyond sublime

there was another journey
in that Mountain that stood before me
let me begin this holy ascent
that i may come to see

the landscapes of my bleakness
and all the lessons learned
i knew there was so much more
for that Fire within still burns

so i gathered all my fortitude
to face this climb ahead
the taxing of this quest to climb
affirms i'm yet not dead

that its self is a blessing
for change in life must come
i am just so thankful, yes
that the Valley is not my Sum

and neither is one Mountain
i pray there's many more
for richness of life is in the journey
not about the score

so . . .

before me stands a Mountain
an this is not the first time
many Valleys more i hope to see
as i embrace my sublime

embracing the sublime . . .

# November 2020 Featured Poets

~ * ~

Elisa Mascia

Sue Lindenberg McClelland

Hatif Janabi

Ivan Gaćina

i Fly because ... said the Dreamer to the world. I Can

# Elisa Mascia

Elisa Mascia, born in Santa Croce di Magliano (Cb), on 13/04/1956, she lives and works in San Giuliano di Puglia (Cb). Retired teacher. Writing is a real need for life and draws inspiration from anything or any surrounding event.

He has participated in various national and international poetry competitions obtaining awards, certificates of participation, merit and honorable mentions. He receives invitations and convocations to multiple international and world events, commemorative and themed events in which he participates.

In July 2019 the first collection of unpublished poems was published in a book entitled "The Grater of the Moon" by the publisher L'inedito Letterario with the editorial by Fabio Martini. […]

# The Poets

Strong emotions
they penetrate the veins.
You assimilate them perfectly,
you make them yours.
They knock you down,
forces are failing.
Touch the bottom.
Go down,
go deep.
Then
in reviving
reasons
no longer with the heart.
Set your soul aside.
Think and understand.
True poets are those who fully convey their emotions.
You who received them,
suffering,
you come back to life.

## Love Trail

In the blue sky
up there the plane that leaves leaves a silver trail ...
and you are the one who looks at the whole world and it is
not enough for you until you see your beloved ...
On the well-defined green lawn with a white robe I am
there to show you the flower of our love ...
the daisy
which gently gives life to our passion.

# Walk under the moon

In a corner of the world
of a cold autumn night
man of the student life,
stars and moon in a circle
all on the ground are waterfalls,
sparkling glitter of diamonds
smiles for the broken hearts,
new hopes are born.
With your hands, a big star,
grabs to be able to follow,
light that never has to fade,
cinnamon expands in the air.
A dream to realize
only if there is love to give,
illuminates everyone's life,
night of stars and moon, it has flourished again.

Sue
Lindenberg
McClelland

# Sue Lindenberg McClelland

Sue McClelland began writing poetry in the early 90's after her divorce. Then she got an MFA in writing fiction. An amateur poet, Sue finds herself writing more and more poetry as she moves towards her eighth decade of life. After 12 years of living with Parkinson's, Sue says, "writing poetry has become an easier and easier way to express and free my mind." Sue is the author of About the Dybbuks: Jewish Historical Fiction from Pittsburgh's Hill District.

## Dad's Birthday

Today you would be 88,
your body turned to ashes
scattered on the ocean
and I am left with memories
left with questions.

I am not afraid to die you said
all yellow and shriveled,
with day-glow teeth
in the greenish florescent lights of the ICU.

I feel you caring
loving me
from the world beyond our world
it always seems as if
you are about to reach
and take me in your lap.

And tell me straight out,
the stories you kept hidden
instead of me having to breathe them in
in white black negatives

You draw me like a compass
my eyes and heart reflecting your position
your umbilicus attaches deep inside me
I feed you still
as if you were my child
and I am here sucking the emptiness
imagining somehow you will reach out
and nourish me

# A Note To Charlie

I watched you planting me a garden
each plant picked with loving care
the Charles Schlesinger Memorial Garden
for me to see when you are not there

It is bittersweet to gaze at them now
then look beside me, empty chair
no jazz pounding out our windows
no New York for us to share

No shady guys, hells angels, policemen
dropping by to pick your brain
your voice as smooth as melted butter
tough and streetwise, soft and sane

As you got weaker, I got stronger
spooned behind you breathing air
here, take my breath, love
you can have some
take some heartbeats I can spare

Buried at Mount Nebo
in a pine box draped with your tallit
the gravestone marks the place we'll both be
shade for you and sun for me

You know what love,
I have a secret
your presence was too large to die
when I get under that rock with you
we'll have fun there you and I

# Hold On Gently, Writing with Wires Unthreading

My words float in the air
and disappear
bubbles from a child's wand
dipped in a plastic jar
of soap suds
I purse my lips and blow through the wand
a shiny bubble quivers in the light
pink and yellow rainbows burst and drop
and burst and drop
a tiny spray of moisture mists my forehead

Is this a benediction?

# Hatif
# Janabi

Hatif Janabi is a bilingual poet, writer, essayist, and translator. He was born in Iraq and is a Polish Citizen. He earned B.A. in Arabic Lang. & Literature from Univ. of Baghdad (1972), M.A. in Polish Lang. & Literature, Univ. of Warsaw (1979) and Ph.D. in Theatre from Warsaw Univ. (1983), where he was a professor of Arabic literature & Culture. He worked in the University of Tizi-Ouzu in Algeria (1985-1988), was Associated Professor in 1987-1988, and a Visiting Scholar, Indiana Univ. (1993-1994) USA.

He is an Author of (33) books of poetry, criticism & translation and a co-author of (15) books and over hundred articles and essays published in various languages. His poems appeared in more than (15) languages including, Arabic, English, French, Chinese, Czech German, Greek, Persian, Polish, Russian, Spanish etc. He is mentioned by literary critics as "One of the prominent contemporary poets & essayist". […]

# Misunderstanding

Spring is late this year with no meaning or cause.
I even forgot myself among the scattered leaves of autumn.
In my homeland, spring is summer's twin;
winter is autumn's neighbor.
We said, life expands and shortens;
an oasis, the villains transformed into an arid wasteland.
Spring shouldn't disappear like water in the sand.
Is it plausible to say this is a forest without trees?
These shores, filled with sands and oysters,
have no sea to contain their banks;
no clouds, stars, or a sun gleam on the bloom of their
cheeks?
Do seasons have a star or a comet to paint their destinies?
Are we meant, my wife, Adam, his dog, and I,
to wear our green clothes,
waiting for a visible or invisible, cunning scene?
 As soon as I remove a bud rom the layer,
I behold a tear flowing over the bud,
swiftly drying in its place.
Spring is too late this year;
a life lost on its way to burgeoning.

Warsaw, May 23, 2012.

*translated by Dr. Khahtan Mandwee*

# So That the Butterfly Won't Die Inside Me*

I dig a hole in the oak of poetry
and open the volcano's mouth
so that the grass burgeons and the roses prickle.
I write so the light, at the tunnel's end, won't die;
the bread loaf cheers the glory of the blood spilled around
it;
the stones have a savor and color,
and the flowers have the kiss's weight.
I write so the friend won't die forever;
no tree bends or bud withers;
no datepalm sinks in the landfill of absence,
no ink or rain or spring dries;
no man despairs,
or a lover's prayer goes to waste.
I write to tell the wind,
"I'm your brother in storm,
the igniter of the first spark,
the keeper of thunder
the guard of the trail."
I write so the words
won't be buried;
the valiant vision won't disappear
in the distraction of sight;
the butterfly won't die
inside me,
and the nightmare of doubts
won't sweep the dream.
I write so no innocent be
slain;
no sinner be stoned;
no child dies
from explosion;

no living-dead are
mutilated;
no other meaning for
water than life;
nor to be like the
caves' inhabitants
or a rotten shoe
riddled by the roads.
 I write so darkness
won't be day.
Babel drinks from the
hand of light;
the river continues to run to the
fields and the plains;
its marks are on the mountains, its
glitter among the clouds.
 I write so my mother's prayer and
father's praise
be the stars' hymn and the clouds'
plea;
the invisible be seen, the inaudible be
heard,
and the untouchable be touched.
 I write to beseech God, "Give me
Your email;
let us frankly talk,
to fathom the savor of
dialogue and
grievance
without a mediator or
a spy."
I write so inhalation and exhalation
have a meaning,
a purpose in life,
and for the beloved to have a statue
higher than the mountains.

I write so that no
seeker is humiliated;
no flower dries up
You'll be me; I'll be
you,
as big as air, water,
and food.
 I write so that the
wing will be as
spacious as its dream,
and the light present, in the might of
its guardian,
floating in the open
space, in us, around
us;
I write to be me.

 Warsaw, June 8,
2011


*translated by Dr. Khuhtan Mandwee*

# Invitation

I won't invite anyone, after now
to my house, inhibited by ghosts
My lock is rusty.
Whoever used to greet me is a pig.
My neighbors are rats.
I won't invite their daughter for fear of the Jinni's king,
sitting behind the door.
I won't invite the dolphin, friend of desolation,
or whoever crawls behind the Sultan's shades.
I won't invite whomever is invited of life's luxuries.
Tonight
I've decided to invite the sea and all its fish
to take me
after the party
to the whale's abdomen
so that I write my life's story
and sing my awaited tune.

June 16, 2014


*translated by Dr. Khahtan Mandwee*

# Ivan Gaćina

# Ivan Gaćina

Ivan Gaćina (Zadar, Croatia) writes poetry, including haiku, short stories, aphorisms, and book reviews. He is the author of three poetry books, *Tebe traži moja rima* (KC Kalliopa, Našice, Croatia, 2014), *Tvorac misli / prolaznik u noći* (SVEN, Niš, Serbia, 2015) and *Okovani prokletstvom* (IK „Rrom produkcija" & Udruženje romskih književnika, Belgrade, Serbia, 2018). Gaćina's works have been published in a number of journals and awarded in many literary contests.

Facebook: https://www.facebook.com/ivan.gacina

Web link: https://www.pesem.si/ivangacina

# Chained by Damnation

The poor stuck
in the tents
in a forgotten
sooty alley.
From all sides
hustle and bustle
of hungry people.
The sound of violin breaks
the night's silence,
uncertainty everywhere.
A blind fortune-teller
predicts the future,
a wooden carriage
waits for better days.
As if time has stopped.
The rich dream of
non-existent
happiness,
chained by damnation,
they live someone else's sins.

# A Home Made of Wind

I travel
from one day to the next,
from one house to another,
from one nightmare
to another.
Far away is my native tent
while I wonder where
and if the future has
anything in store for me.
My wife
travels with me and on her own,
with children and without them,
with the sadness in her soul
and full of hope for a better life.
Maybe we will meet
once in a dream
there where, instead of hope,
a home made of wind
waits for us and
carries us with it.

Ivan Gaćina

# Daybreak on Zvezdara

In Veliki Vračar
entangled with Zvezdara
stars meet and,
with their light,
crown Belgrade avenues,
a criss-cross of paths
of human destinies.
Through the song of nightingales
the smell of coffee
surpasses in the glossy beauty
the Lipov Lad restaurant
while the waters of the Pasha's Fountain
carry away the unspoken wishes.
In the shade of
the sacred plane tree
an old Gypsy woman
sells extinct memories,
shards of the stars
exposing
the dawn of civilization.

# Remembering

## our fallen soldiers of verse

*Janet Perkins Caldwell*

February 14, 1959 ~ September 20, 2016

*Alan W. Jankowski*

16 March 1961 ~ 10 March 2017

*Now available*

1 April 2020

World Healing World Peace
2020

Poets for Humanity

# Inner Child Press

# News

## Poetry Posse Members

We are so excited to share and announce a few of the current books, as well as the new and upcoming books of some of our Poetry Posse authors.

On the following pages we present to you ...

Jackie Davis Allen

Gail Weston Shazor

hülya n. yılmaz

Nizar Sartawi

Faleeha Hassan

Fahredin Shehu

Caroline 'Ceri' Nazareno

Eliza Segiet

Teresa E. Gallion

William S. Peters, Sr.

Now Available at
www.innerchildpress.com

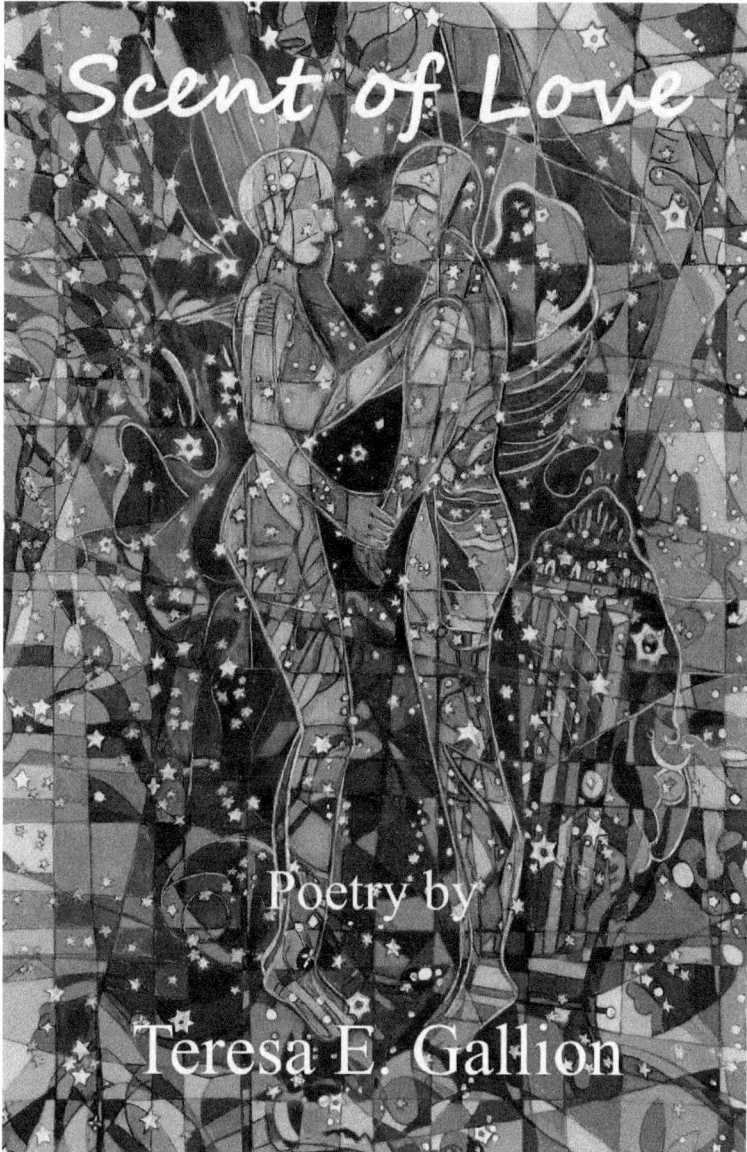

Scent of Love

Poetry by

Teresa E. Gallion

*Now Available*

*www.innerchildpress.com*

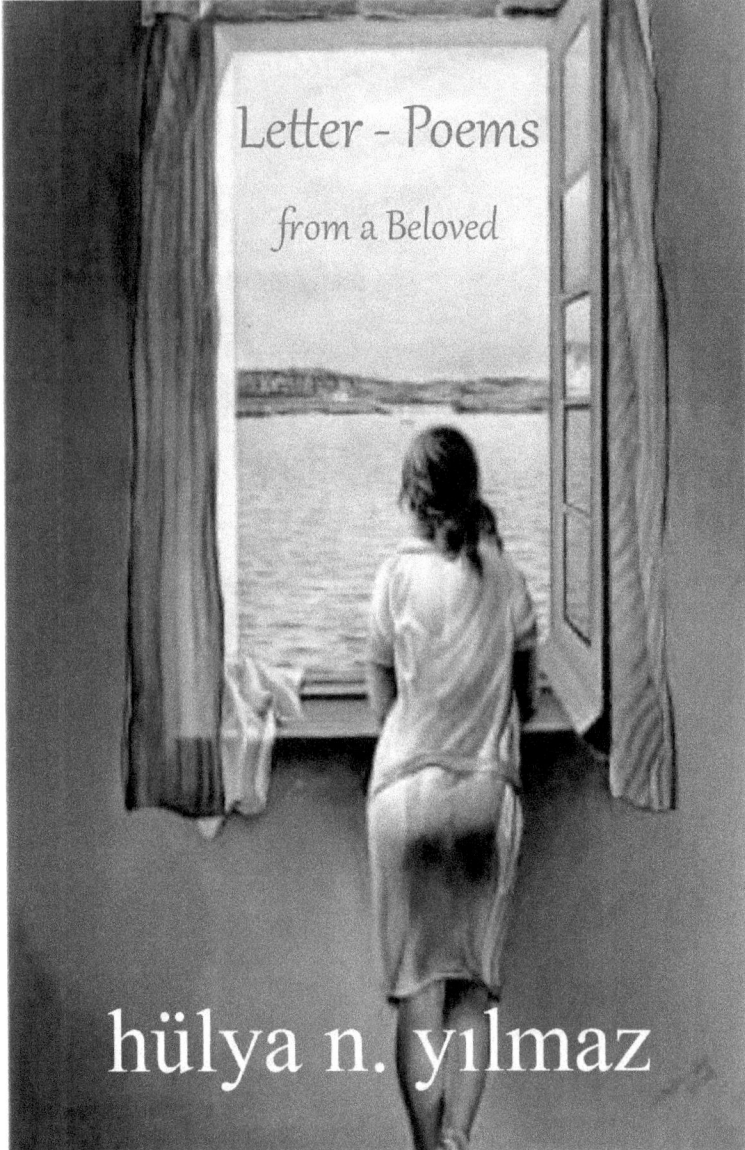

Letter - Poems

from a Beloved

hülya n. yılmaz

Now Available

www.innerchildpress.com

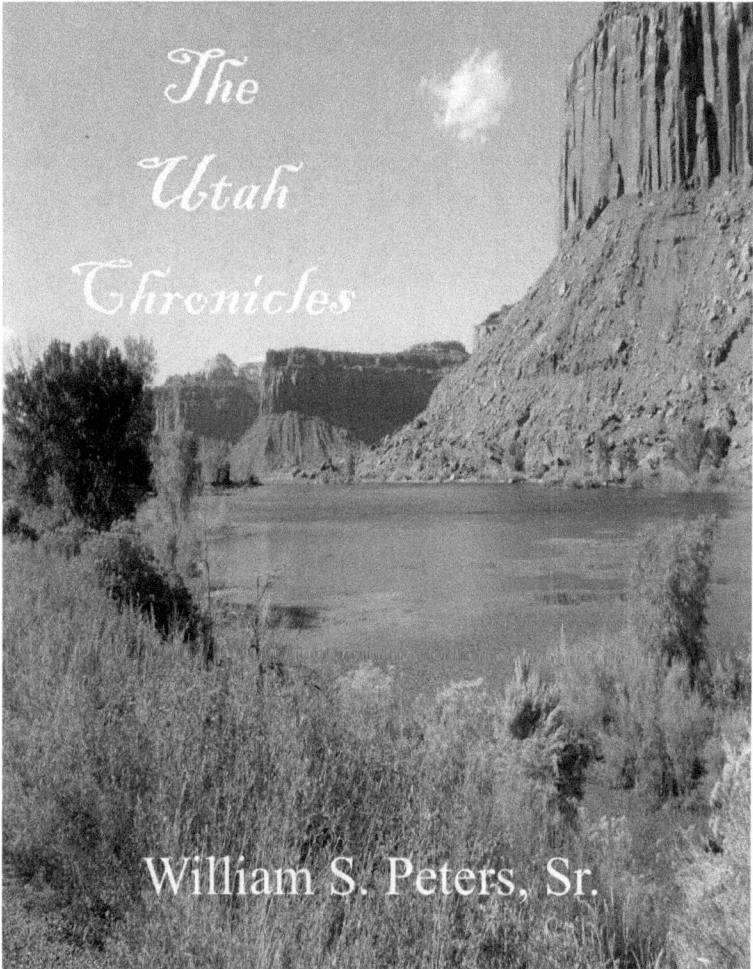

The
Utah
Chronicles

William S. Peters, Sr.

Now Available

www.innerchildpress.com

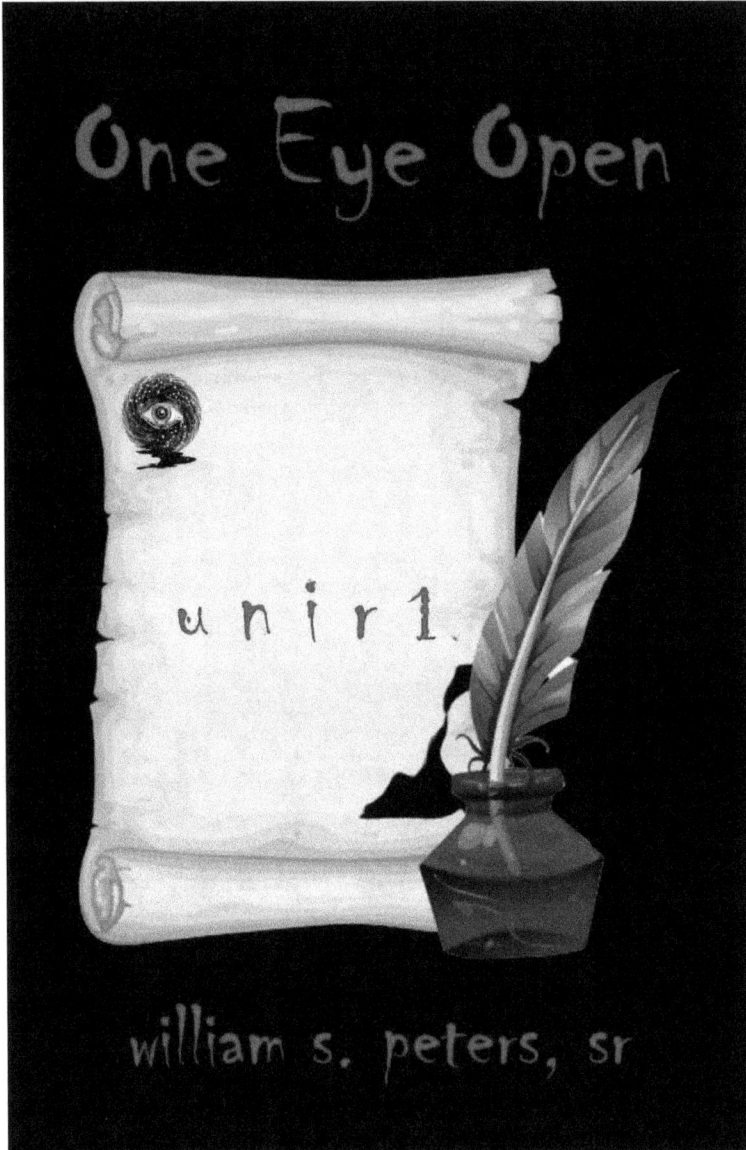

# COMING SOON

www.innerchildpress.com

# The Book of krisar

## volume v

## william s. peters, sr.

## Now Available
www.innerchildpress.com

# The Book of krisar

### Volume I

william s. peters, sr.

# The Book of krisar

### Volume II

william s. peters, sr.

*Now Available*

www.innerchildpress.com

# The Book of krisar

## Volume III

## william s. peters, sr.

# The Book of krisar

## Volume IV

## william s. peters, sr.

Now Available

www.innerchildpress.com

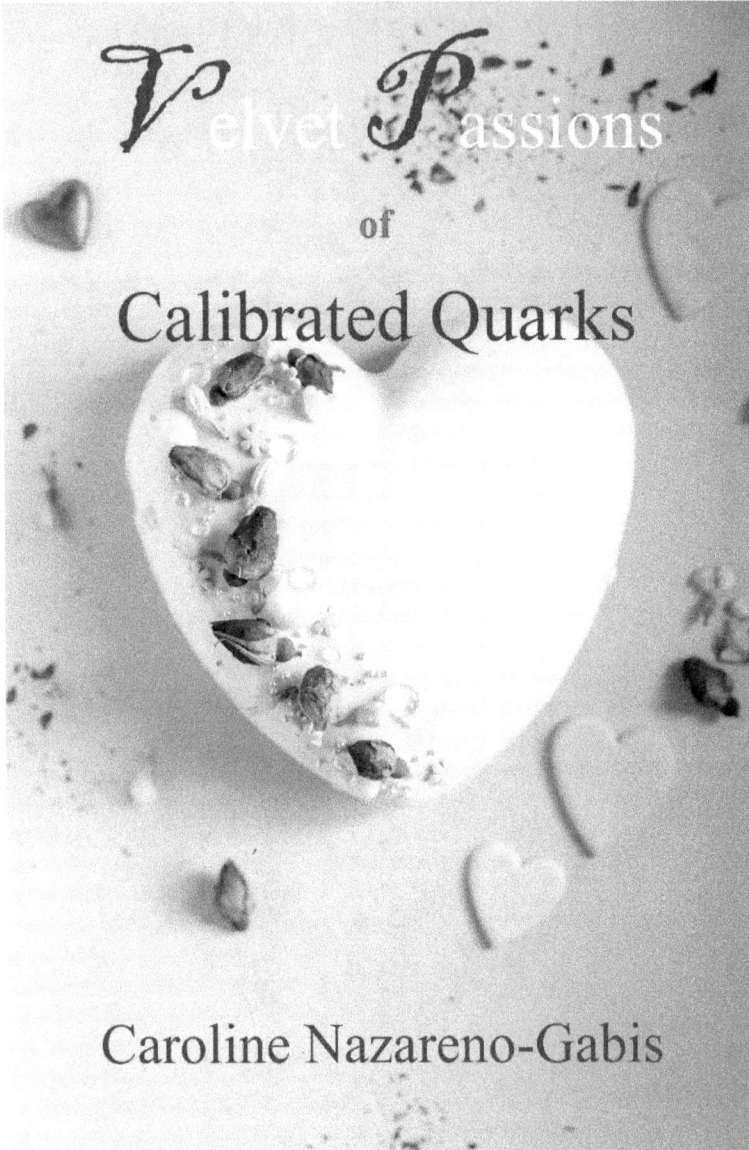

Velvet Passions

of

Calibrated Quarks

Caroline Nazareno-Gabis

*Now Available*

www.innerchildpress.com

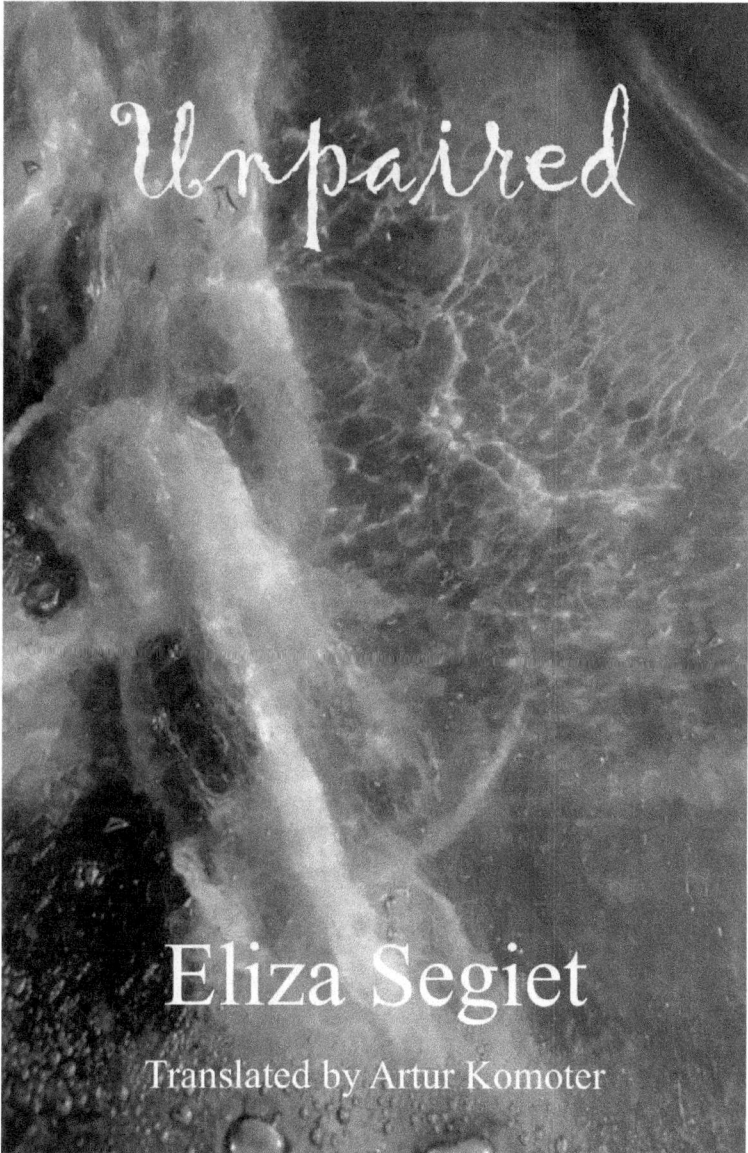

Unpaired

Eliza Segiet

Translated by Artur Komoter

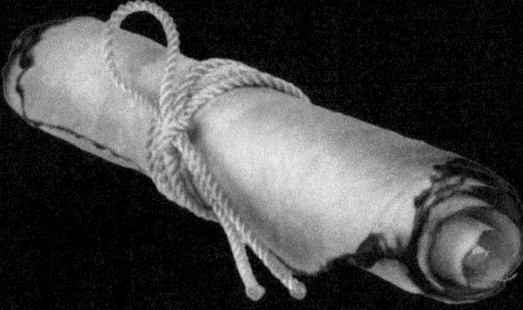

Canlarım

My Lifeblood

*poetry in Turkish and English*

hülya n. yılmaz

*Now Available*

www.innerchildpress.com

Butterfly's Voice

Faleeha Hassan

Translated by William M. Hutchins

*Now Available at*

*www.innerchildpress.com*

# No Illusions

*Through the Looking Glass*

Jackie Davis Allen

Now Available at
www.innerchildpress.com

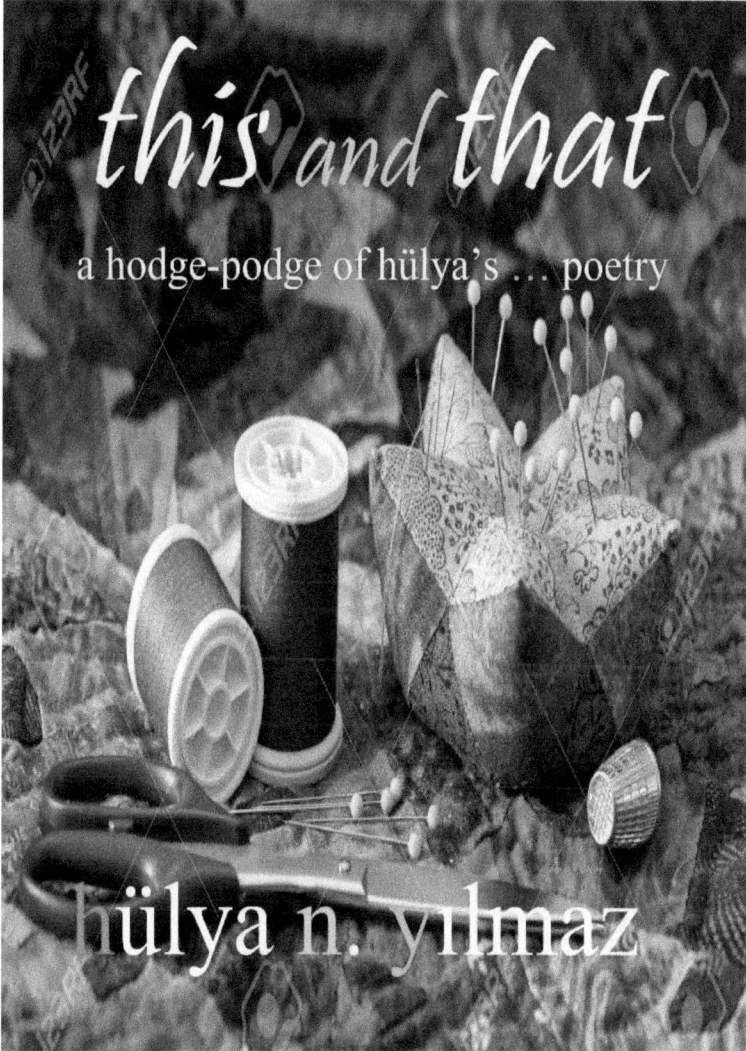

this and that

a hodge-podge of hülya's ... poetry

hülya n. yılmaz

## Now Available at
### www.innerchildpress.com

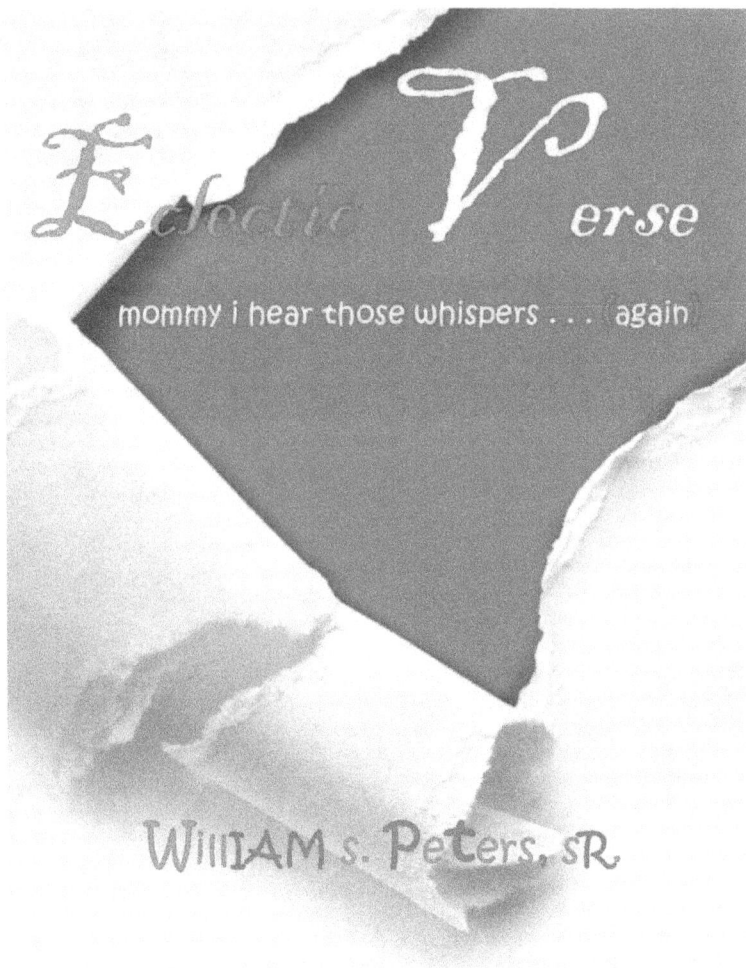

Eclectic Verse

mommy i hear those whispers . . . again

William S. Peters, Sr.

*Now Available at*
<u>*www.innerchildpress.com*</u>

# HERENOW

FAHREDIN SHEHU

*Now Available at*
*www.innerchildpress.com*

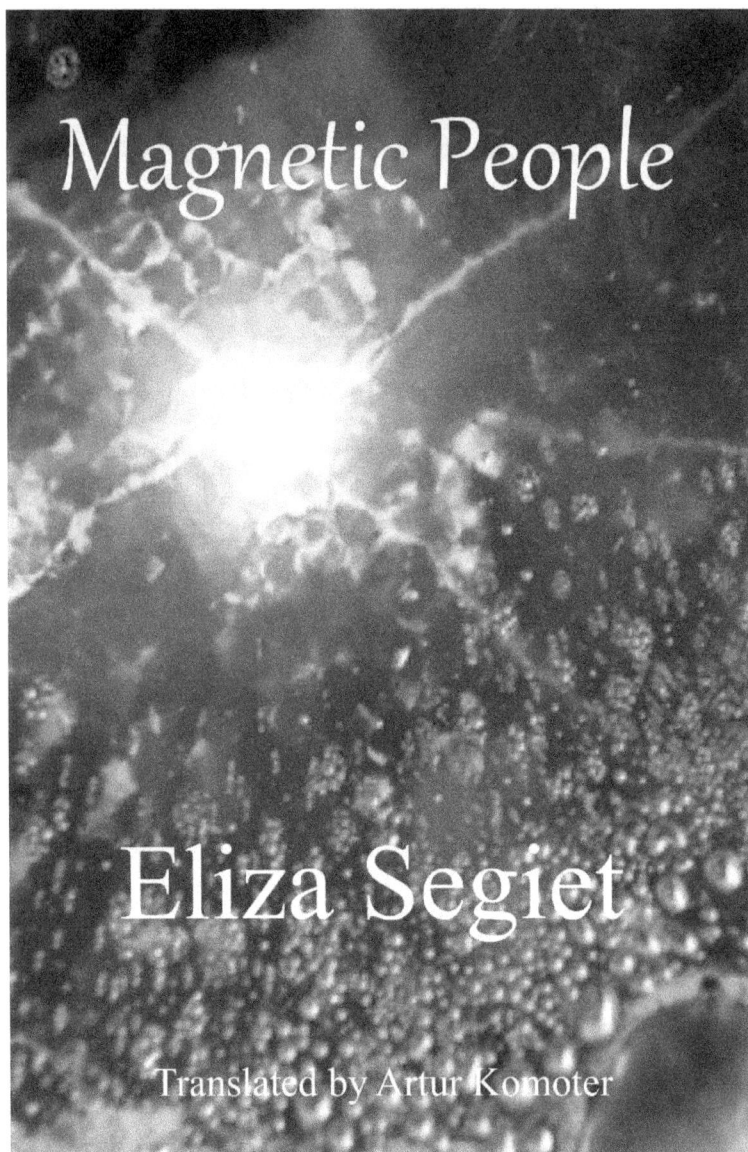

# Magnetic People

## Eliza Segiet

### Translated by Artur Komoter

*Now Available at*
[www.innerchildpress.com](www.innerchildpress.com)

Dark Side

of the

Moon

Jackie Davis Allen

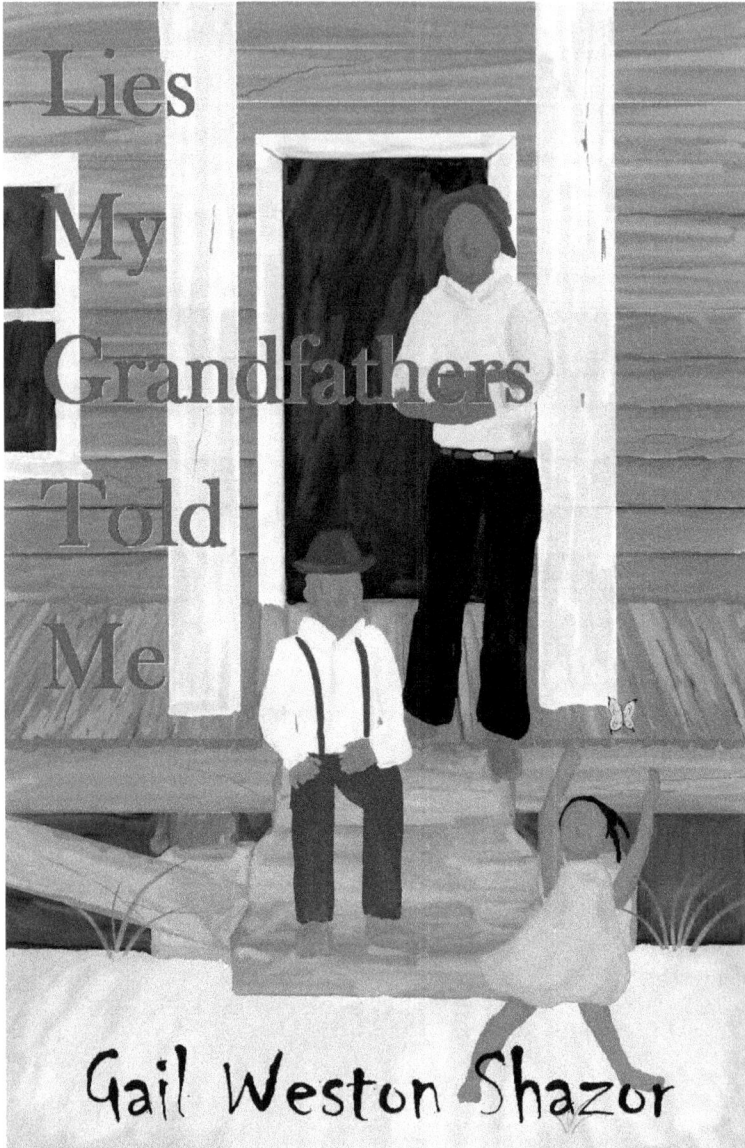

Lies My Grandfathers Told Me

Gail Weston Shazor

Now Available at
www.innerchildpress.com

Aflame

Memoirs in Verse

hülya n. yılmaz

*Now Available at*
*www.innerchildpress.com*

My Shadow

Nizar Sartawi

Now Available at
www.innerchildpress.com

Mass Graves

Faleeha Hassan

*Inner Child Press News*

**Now Available at**
www.innerchildpress.com

# Breakfast

for

# Butterflies

## Faleeha Hassan

*Now Available at*
www.innerchildpress.com

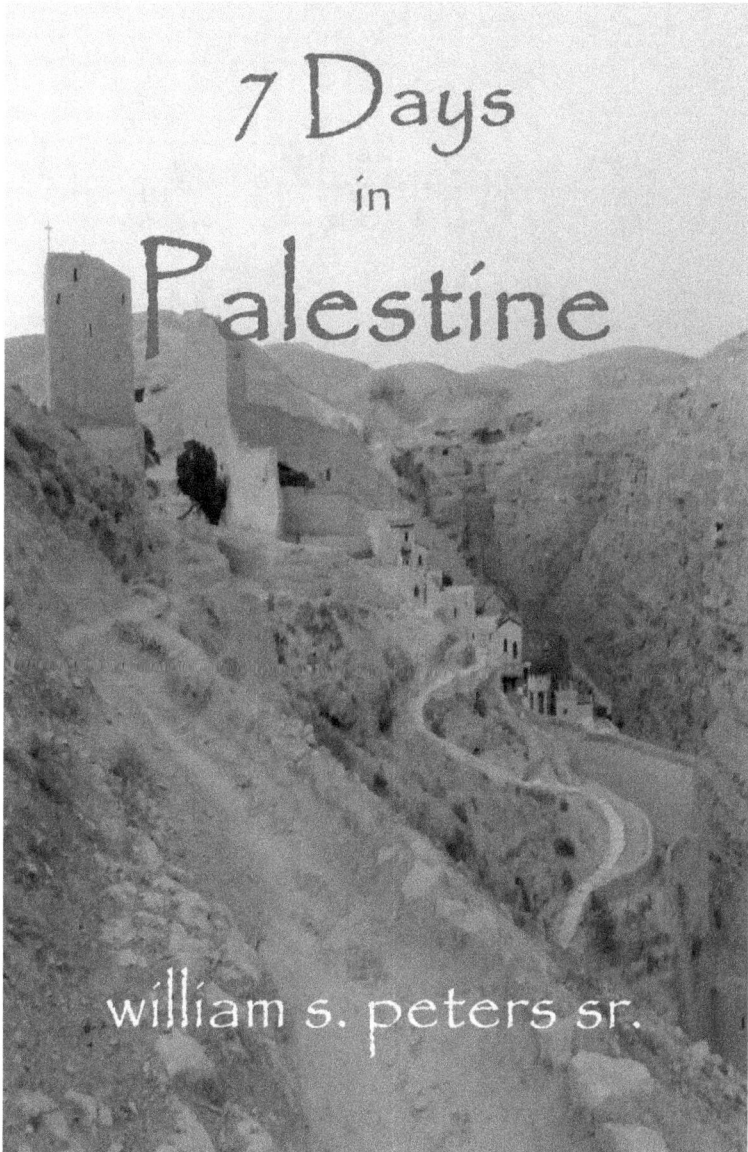

7 Days
in
Palestine

william s. peters sr.

*Now Available at*
*www.innerchildpress.com*

inner child press
presents

*Tunisia My Love*

william s. peters, sr.

Now Available at
www.innerchildpress.com

INNER CHILD PRESS

THIS IS WHY I
SLEEP

william s. peters sr.

## Now Available at
## www.innerchildpress.com

Think on These Things
Book II

# william s. peters, sr.

# Other

## Anthological

### works from

Inner Child Press International

www.innerchildpress.com

World Healing World Peace
2020

Poets for Humanity

*Now Available*

www.worldhealingworldpeacepoetry.com

Inner Child Press International
&
The Year of the Poet
present

# Poetry

*the best of 2020*

# Poets of the World

*Coming December 2020*
*www.innerchildpress.com*

Inner Child Press International

*presents*

# W.A.R.

## We Are Revolution

*Poets for Humanity*

*Now Available*

*www.innerchildpress.com*

the Heart of a Poet

words for a better tomorrow

## The Conscious Poets

*Now Available*

*www.innerchildpress.com*

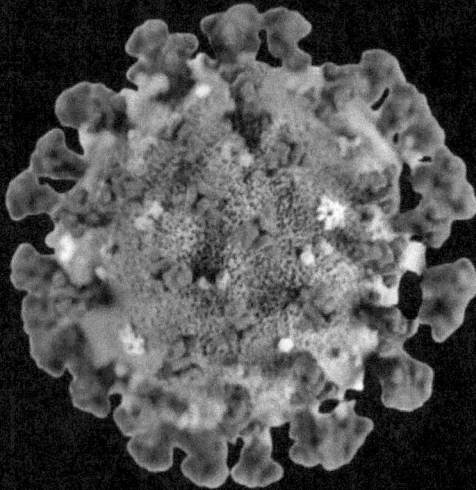

Poetry

from the

Balkans

The Balkan Poets

*Now Available at*

*www.innerchildpress.com*

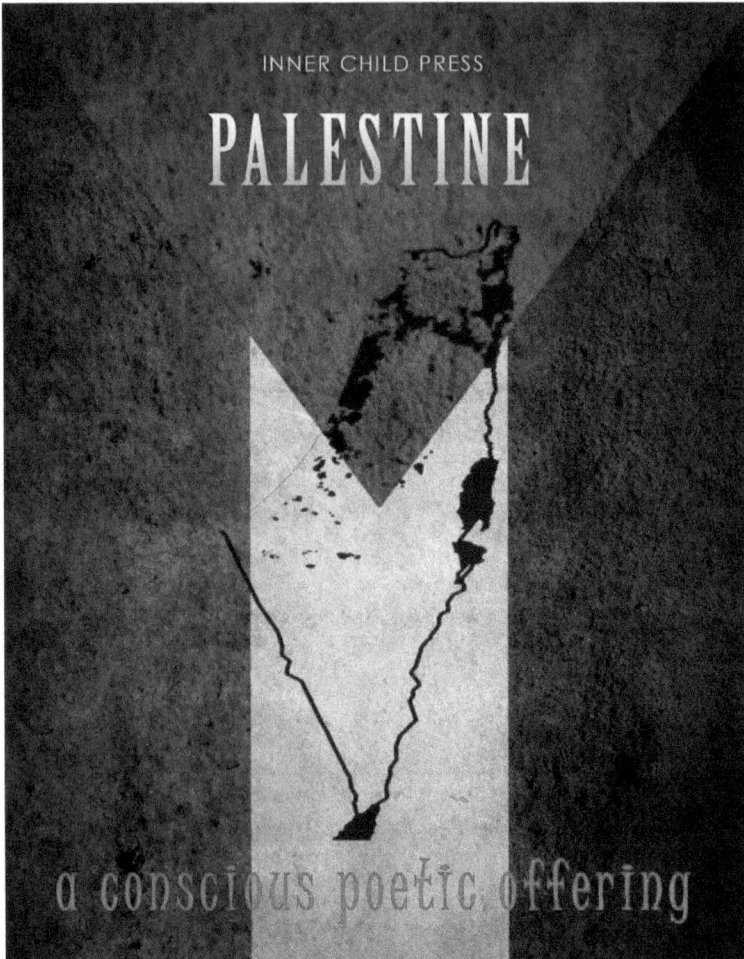

*Now Available at*
*www.innerchildpress.com*

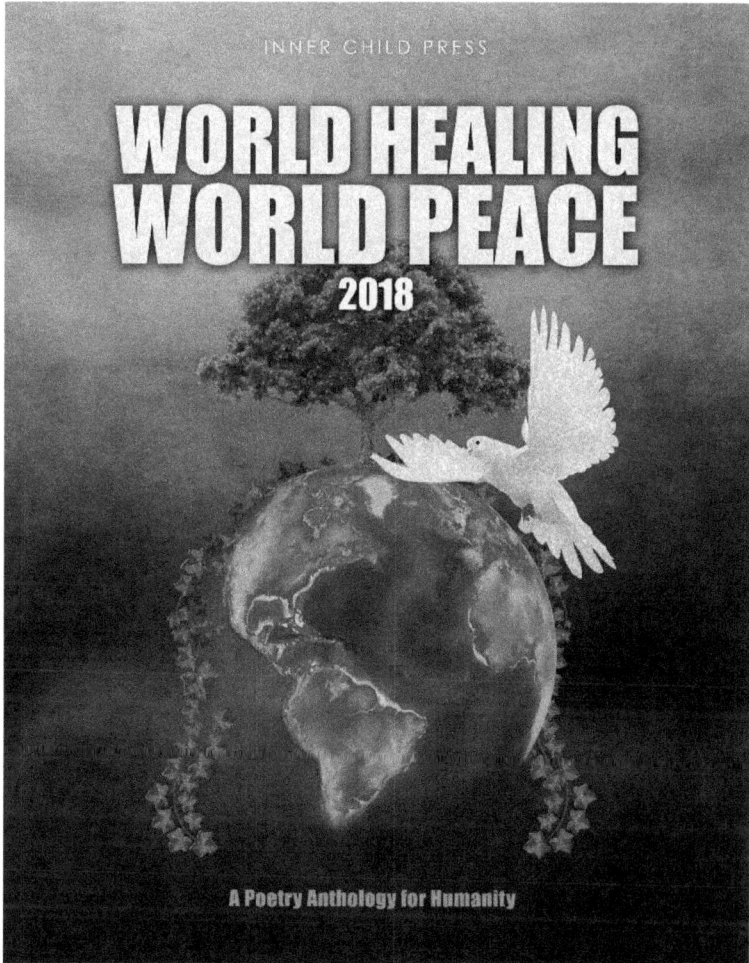

*Now Available at*
*www.innerchildpress.com*

Inner Child Press International
*presents*

A Love Anthology
2019

The Love Poets

*Now Available*

www.worldhealingworldpeacepoetry.com

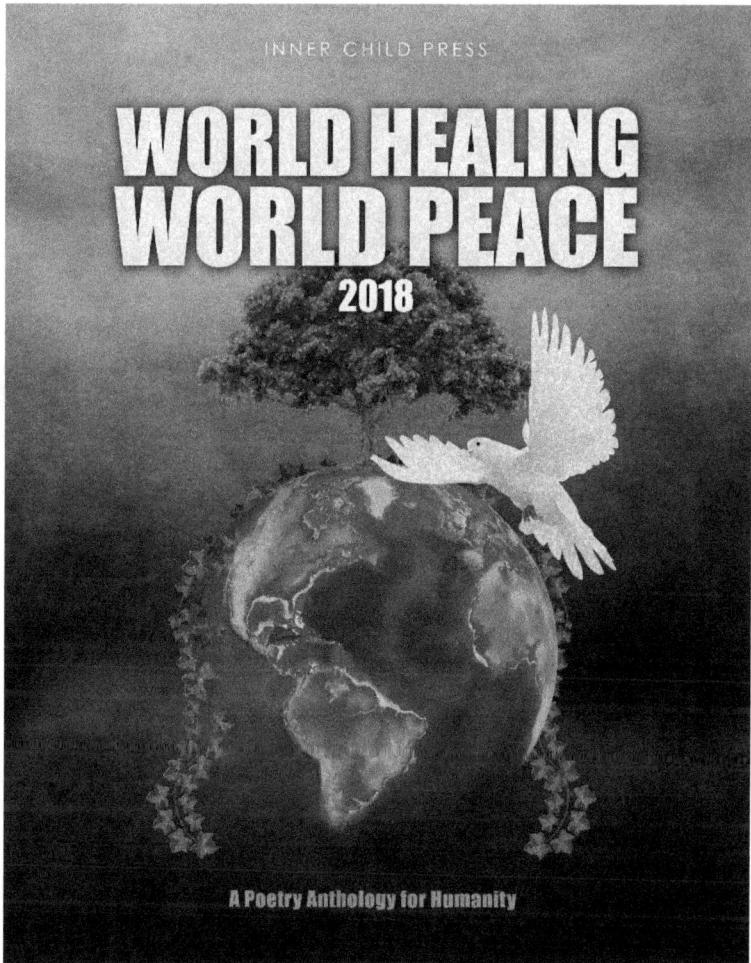

Now Available

www.worldhealingworldpeacepoetry.com

**World Healing World Peace**

INNER CHILD PRESS
**World Healing World Peace**
A Poetry Anthology 2014
*Volume 1*

INNER CHILD PRESS
**World Healing World Peace**
A Poetry Anthology 2014
*Volume 2*

**World Healing World Peace**
A POETRY ANTHOLOGY
*Volume 1*

**World Healing World Peace**
A POETRY ANTHOLOGY
*Volume 2*

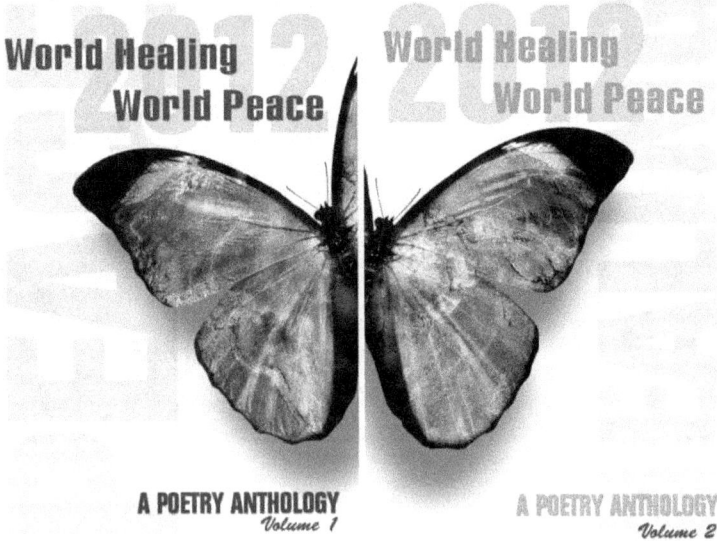

*Now Available*

www.worldhealingworldpeacepoetry.com

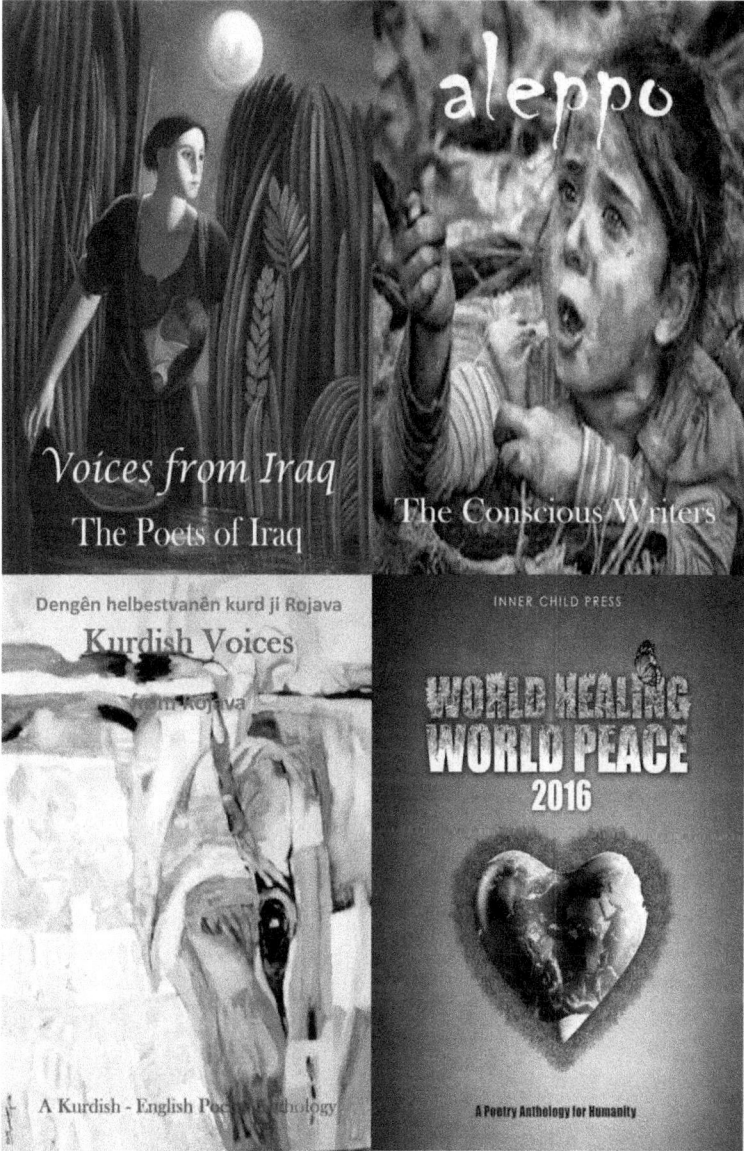

*Now Available*

www.innerchildpress.com/anthologies

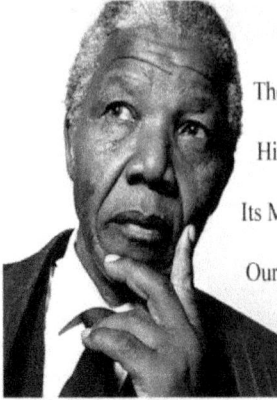

# Mandela

The Man

His Life

Its Meaning

Our Words

Poetry . . . Commentary & Stories
*The Anthological Writers*

## A GATHERING OF WORDS

POETRY & COMMENTARY
FOR
**TRAYVON MARTIN**

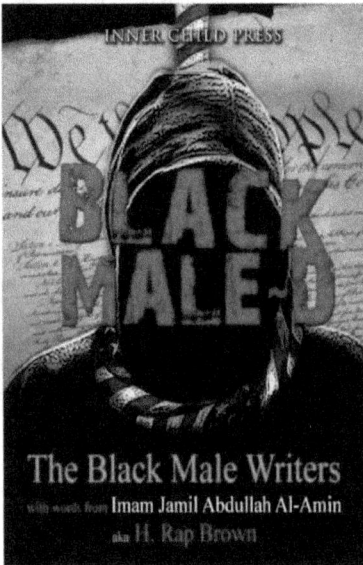

The Black Male Writers
with words from Imam Jamil Abdullah Al-Amin
aka H. Rap Brown

I want my poetry to... *volume* 4

the conscious poets
*inspired by* . . . Monte Smith

*Now Available*

www.innerchildpress.com/anthologies

Now Available

www.innerchildpress.com/anthologies

healing through words

Poetry ... Prose ... Prayer ... Stories

Janet
gone too soon . . .

a
Poetically
Spoken
Anthology
volume 1
Collector's Edition

The Poetry Posse
Presents

an anthology
of

Love

The Poetry Posse 2016

Now Available

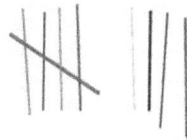

## Now Available

www.innerchildpress.com/anthologies

## The Year of the Poet
### January 2014

The Poetry Posse

Jamie Bond
Gail Weston Shazor
Albert 'Infinite' Carrasco
Siddartha Beth Pierce
Janet P. Caldwell
June 'Bugg' Barefield
Debbie M. Allen
Tony Henninger
Joe DaVerbal Minddancer
Robert Gibbons
Neetu Wali
Shareef Abdur-Rasheed
William S. Peters, Sr.

Carnation

*Our January Feature*
**Terri L. Johnson**

## the Year of the Poet
### February 2014

violets

The Poetry Posse

Jamie Bond
Gail Weston Shazor
Albert 'Infinite' Carrasco
Siddartha Beth Pierce
Janet P. Caldwell
June 'Bugg' Barefield
Debbie M. Allen
Tony Henninger
Joe DaVerbal Minddancer
Robert Gibbons
Neetu Wali
Shareef Abdur-Rasheed
William S. Peters, Sr.

*Our February Features*
**Teresa E. Gallion & Robert Gibson**

## the Year of the Poet
### March 2014

The Poetry Posse

Jamie Bond
Gail Weston Shazor
Albert 'Infinite' Carrasco
Siddartha Beth Pierce
Janet P. Caldwell
June 'Bugg' Barefield
Debbie M. Allen
Tony Henninger
Joe DaVerbal Minddancer
Robert Gibbons
Neetu Wali
Shareef Abdur-Rasheed
Kimberly Burnham
William S. Peters, Sr.

daffodil

*Our March Featured Poets*
Alicia C. Cooper & Hülya Yılmaz

## the Year of the Poet
### April 2014

The Poetry Posse

Jamie Bond
Gail Weston Shazor
Albert 'Infinite' Carrasco
Siddartha Beth Pierce
Janet P. Caldwell
June 'Bugg' Barefield
Debbie M. Allen
Tony Henninger
Joe DaVerbal Minddancer
Robert Gibbons
Neetu Wali
Shareef Abdur-Rasheed
Kimberly Burnham
William S. Peters, Sr.

*Our April Featured Poets*
Fahredin Shehu
Martina Reisz Newberry
Justin Blackburn
Monte Smith

Sweet Pea

celebrating international poetry month

# Now Available

www.innerchildpress.com/the-year-of-the-poet

the year of the poet
May 2014

May's Featured Poets
RecCee
Joski the Poet
Shannon Stanton

Dedicated to our Children

The Poetry Posse
Jessie Bond
Gail Weston Shazor
Albert Infinite' Carrasco
Siddartha Beth Pierce
Janet P. Caldwell
June 'Bugg' Barefield
Debbie M. Allen
Tony Henninger
Joe DaVerbal Minddancer
Robert Gibbons
Neetu Wali
Shareef Abdur-Rasheed
Kimberly Burnham
William S. Peters, Sr.

Lily of the Valley

the Year of the Poet
June 2014

Love & Relationship

Rose

June's Featured Poets
Shantelle McLin
Jacqueline D. E. Kennedy
Abraham N. Benjamin

The Poetry Posse
Jessie Bond
Gail Weston Shazor
Albert Infinite' Carrasco
Siddartha Beth Pierce
Janet P. Caldwell
June Bugg Barefield
Debbie M. Allen
Tony Henninger
Joe DaVerbal Minddancer
Robert Gibbons
Neetu Wali
Shareef Abdur-Rasheed
Kimberly Burnham
William S. Peters, Sr.

The Year of the Poet
July 2014

July Feature Poets
Christeene A.V. Williams
Dr. Jolyn R. Shirin
Rolande Otonrewashi Freedom

The Poetry Posse
Jessie Bond
Gail Weston Shazor
Siddartha Beth Pierce
Janet P. Caldwell
June 'Bugg' Barefield
Debbie M. Allen
Tony Henninger
Joe DaVerbal Minddancer
Robert Gibbons
Neetu Wali
Shareef Abdur-Rasheed
Kimberly Burnham
William S. Peters, Sr.

Lotus
Asian Flower of the Month

The Year of the Poet
August 2014

Gladiolus

The Poetry Posse
Jessie Bond
Gail Weston Shazor
Albert Infinite' Carrasco
Siddartha Beth Pierce
Janet P. Caldwell
June 'Bugg' Barefield
Debbie M. Allen
Tony Henninger
Joe DaVerbal Minddancer
Robert Gibbons
Neetu Wali
Shareef Abdur-Rasheed
Kimberly Burnham
William S. Peters, Sr.

August Feature Poets
Ann White ✦ Rosalind Cherry ✦ Shelja Jenkins

Now Available

www.innerchildpress.com/the-year-of-the-poet

183

THE YEAR OF THE POET II
January 2015

Garnet

The Poetry Posse

Jamie Bond
Gail Weston Shazor
Albert 'Infinite' Carrasco
Siddartha Beth Pierce
Janet P. Caldwell
Tony Henninger
Joe DaVerbal Minddancer
Robert Gibbons
Neetu Wali
Shareef Abdur - Rasheed
Kimberly Burnham
Ann White
Keith Alan Hamilton
Katherine Wyatt
Fahredin Shehu
Hülya N. Yılmaz
Teresa E. Gallion
Jackie Allen
William S. Peters, Sr.

January Feature Poets
Bismay Mohanti * Jen Walls * Eric Judah

THE YEAR OF THE POET II
February 2015

Amethyst

THE POETRY POSSE

Jamie Bond
Gail Weston Shazor
Albert 'Infinite' Carrasco
Siddartha Beth Pierce
Janet P. Caldwell
Tony Henninger
Joe DaVerbal Minddancer
Robert Gibbons
Neetu Wali
Shareef Abdur - Rasheed
Kimberly Burnham
Ann White
Keith Alan Hamilton
Katherine Wyatt
Fahredin Shehu
Hülya N. Yılmaz
Teresa E. Gallion
Jackie Allen
William S. Peters, Sr.

FEBRUARY FEATURE POETS
Iram Fatima * Bob McNeil * Kerstin Centervall

The Year of the Poet II
March 2015

Our Featured Poets
Heung Sook * Anthony Arnold * Alicia Poland

Bloodstone

The Poetry Posse 2015
Jamie Bond * Gail Weston Shazor * Albert 'Infinite' Carrasco
Siddartha Beth Pierce * Janet P. Caldwell * Tony Henninger
Joe DaVerbal Minddancer * Neetu Wali * Shareef Abdur – Rasheed
Kimberly Burnham * Ann White * Keith Alan Hamilton
Katherine Wyatt * Fahredin Shehu * Hülya N. Yılmaz
Teresa E. Gallion * Jackie Allen * William S. Peters, Sr.

The Year of the Poet II
April 2015
Celebrating International Poetry Month

Our Featured Poets
Raja Williams * Dennis Ferado * Laure Charazac

Diamonds

The Poetry Posse 2015
Jamie Bond * Gail Weston Shazor * Albert 'Infinite' Carrasco
Siddartha Beth Pierce * Janet P. Caldwell * Tony Henninger
Joe DaVerbal Minddancer * Neetu Wali * Shareef Abdur – Rasheed
Kimberly Burnham * Ann White * Keith Alan Hamilton
Katherine Wyatt * Fahredin Shehu * Hülya N. Yılmaz
Teresa E. Gallion * Jackie Allen * William S. Peters, Sr.

Now Available

www.innerchildpress.com/the-year-of-the-poet

## The Year of the Poet II
### May 2015

May's Featured Poets
Geri Algeri
Akin Mosi Chimeny
Anna Jakubcza

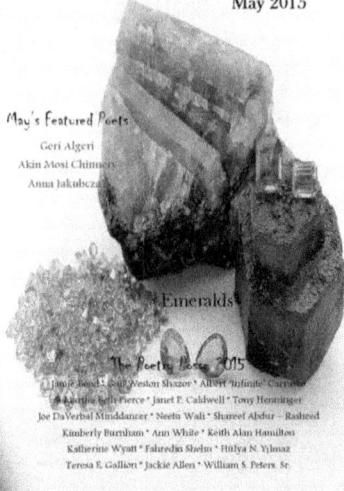

Emeralds

The Poetry Posse 2015
Jamie Bond * Gail Weston Shazor * Albert 'Infinite' Carrasco
Siddartha Beth Pierce * Janet P. Caldwell * Tony Henninger
Joe DaVerbal Minddancer * Neetu Wali * Shareef Abdur - Rasheed
Kimberly Burnham * Ann White * Keith Alan Hamilton
Katherine Wyatt * Fahredin Shehu * Hülya N. Yılmaz
Teresa E. Gallion * Jackie Allen * William S. Peters, Sr.

## The Year of the Poet II
### June 2015

June's Featured Poets
Anahit Arustamyan * Yvette D. Murrell * Regina A. Walker

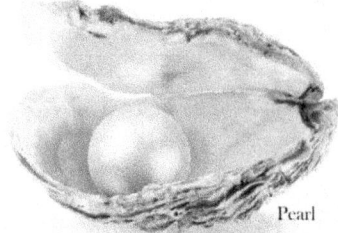

Pearl

The Poetry Posse 2015
Jamie Bond * Gail Weston Shazor * Albert 'Infinite' Carrasco
Siddartha Beth Pierce * Janet P. Caldwell * Tony Henninger
Joe DaVerbal Minddancer * Neetu Wali * Shareef Abdur - Rasheed
Kimberly Burnham * Ann White * Keith Alan Hamilton
Katherine Wyatt * Fahredin Shehu * Hülya N. Yılmaz
Teresa E. Gallion * Jackie Allen * William S. Peters, Sr

## The Year of the Poet II
### July 2015

The Featured Poets for July 2015
Abhik Shome * Christina Neal * Robert Neal

Rubies

The Poetry Posse 2015
Jamie Bond * Gail Weston Shazor * Albert 'Infinite' Carrasco
Siddartha Beth Pierce * Janet P. Caldwell * Tony Henninger
Joe DaVerbal Minddancer * Neetu Wali * Shareef Abdur - Rasheed
Kimberly Burnham * Ann White * Keith Alan Hamilton
Katherine Wyatt * Fahredin Shehu * Hülya N. Yılmaz
Teresa E. Gallion * Jackie Allen * William S. Peters, Sr.

## The Year of the Poet II
### August 2015

Peridot

Featured Poets
Gayle Howell
Ann Chalasz
Christopher Schultz

The Poetry Posse 2015
Jamie Bond * Gail Weston Shazor * Albert 'Infinite' Carrasco
Siddartha Beth Pierce * Janet P. Caldwell * Tony Henninger
Joe DaVerbal Minddancer * Neetu Wali * Shareef Abdur - Rasheed
Kimberly Burnham * Ann White * Keith Alan Hamilton
Katherine Wyatt * Fahredin Shehu * Hülya N. Yılmaz
Teresa E. Gallion * Jackie Allen * William S. Peters, Sr

## Now Available

www.innerchildpress.com/the-year-of-the-poet

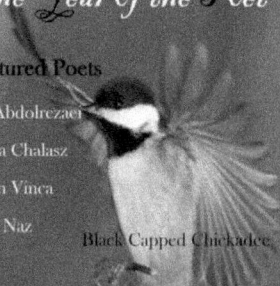

The Year of the Poet III
January 2016

Featured Poets

Lana Joseph * Atom Cyrus Rush * Christena Williams

Dark-eyed Junco

The Poetry Posse 2016

The Year of the Poet III
February 2016

Featured Poets

Anthony Arnold
Anna Chalasz
Jon Andre Hawthorne

Puffin

The Poetry Posse 2016

The Year of the Poet
March 2016

Featured Poets

Jeton Kelmendi    Nizar Sartawi    Sami Muhanna

Robin

The Poetry Posse 2016

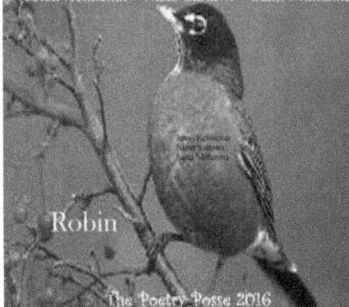

The Year of the Poet III

Featured Poets

Ali Abdolrezaei

Anna Chalasz

Agim Vinca

Ceri Naz

Black Capped Chickadee

The Poetry Posse 2016

celebrating international poetry month

# Now Available

www.innerchildpress.com/the-year-of-the-poet

The Year of the Poet
May 2016

Bob Strum
Barbara Allan
D.L. Davis

Oriole

The Year of the Poet III
June 2016

Featured Poets

Qibrije Demiri- Frangu
Naime Beqiraj
Faleeha Hassan
Bedri Zyberaj

Black Necked Stilt

The Poetry Posse 2016

The Year of the Poet III
July 2016

Tram Fatima 'Ashi'
Langley Shazor
Jody Doty
Emilia T. Davis

Indigo Bunting

The Poetry Posse 2016

The Year of the Poet III
August 2016

Featured Poets

Anita Dash
Irena Jovanovic
Malgorzata Gouluda

Painted Bunting

The Poetry Posse 2016

Now Available

www.innerchildpress.com/the-year-of-the-poet

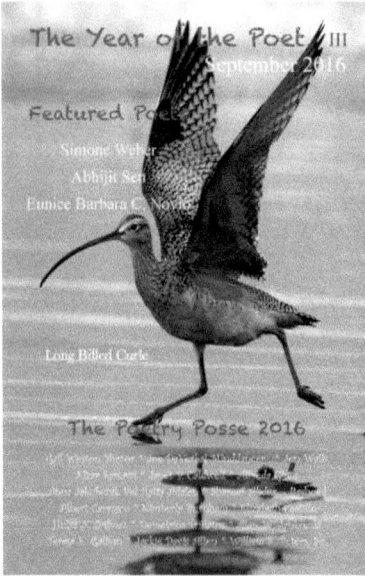

The Year of the Poet III
September 2016

Featured Poets

Simone Weber
Abhijit Sen
Eunice Barbara C. Novio

Long Billed Curle

The Poetry Posse 2016

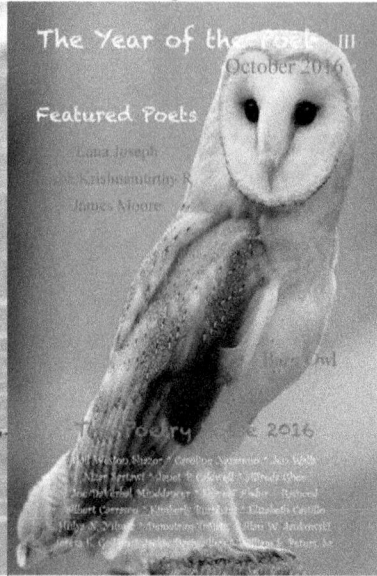

The Year of the Poet III
October 2016

Featured Poets

Lana Joseph
Krishnamurtiny
James Moore

Barn Owl

The Poetry Posse 2016

The Year of the Poet III
November 2016

Featured Poets

Rosemary Burns
Robin Ouzman Hislop
Lonneice Weeks-Badley

Northern Cardinal

The Poetry Posse 2016

Gail Weston Shazor * Caroline Nazareno * Jen Walls
Nizar Sartawi * Janet P. Caldwell * Alfreda Ghee
Joe DaVerbal Minddancer * Shareef Abdur - Rasheed
Albert Carrasco * Kimberly Burnham * Elizabeth Castillo
Hülya N. Yılmaz * Demetrios Trifiatis * Alan W. Jankowski
Teresa E. Gallion * Jackie Davis Allen * William S. Peters, Sr

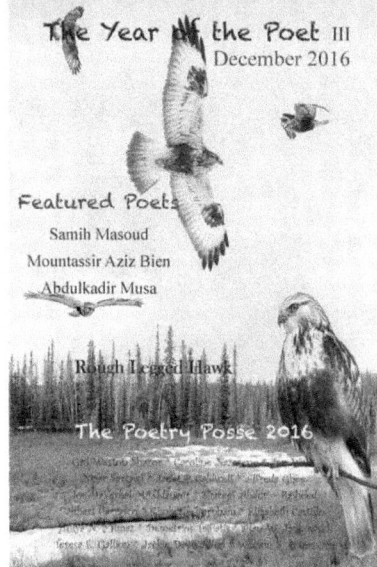

The Year of the Poet III
December 2016

Featured Poets

Samih Masoud
Mountassir Aziz Bien
Abdulkadir Musa

Rough Legged Hawk

The Poetry Posse 2016

# Now Available

www.innerchildpress.com/the-year-of-the-poet

The Year of the Poet IV
January 2017

Featured Poets
Jon Vinell
Natalie Shields
Irani Fatima 'Ashi

Quaking Aspen

The Poetry Posse 2017

Gail Weston Shazor * Caroline Nazareno * Jhimmy Mohroty
Nizar Sartawi * Anna Jakubczak Vel Ratty Adalan * Jen Walls
Joe DaVerbal Minddancer * Shareef Abdur - Rasheed
Albert Carrasco * Kimberly Burnham * Elizabeth Castillo
Hülya N. Yılmaz * Teloshu Hasan * Alan W. Jankowski
Teresa E. Gallion * Jackie Davis Allen * William S. Peters, Sr.

The Year of the Poet IV
February 2017

Featured Poets
Lin Ross
Sonkatna Fathi
Gewer Gitani

Witch Hazel

The Poetry Posse 2017

Gail Weston Shazor * Caroline Nazareno * Jhimmy Mohroty
Nizar Sartawi * Anna Jakubczak Vel Ratty Adalan * Jen Walls
Joe DaVerbal Minddancer * Shareef Abdur - Rasheed
Albert Carrasco * Kimberly Burnham * Elizabeth Castillo
Hülya N. Yılmaz * Teloshu Hasan * Alan W. Jankowski
Teresa E. Gallion * Jackie Davis Allen * William S. Peters, Sr.

The Year of the Poet IV
March 2017

Featured Poets
Tremell Stevens
Francisca Ricinski
Jamit Abu Shaih

The Eastern Redbud

The Poetry Posse 2017

Gail Weston Shazor * Caroline Nazareno * Jhimmy Mohroty
Teresa E. Gallion * Anna Jakubczak Vel Ratty Adalan
Joe DaVerbal Minddancer * Shareef Abdur - Rasheed
Albert Carrasco * Kimberly Burnham * Elizabeth Castillo
Hülya N. Yılmaz * Teloshu Hasan * Jackie Davis Allen
Jen Walls * Nizar Sartawi * * William S. Peters, Sr.

The Year of the Poet IV
April 2017

Featured Poets
Dr. Rachida Barman
Neptune Barman
Masood Khahf

The Blossoming Cherry

The Poetry Posse 2017

Gail Weston Shazor * Caroline Nazareno * Jhimmy Mohroty

*Now Available*

www.innerchildpress.com/the-year-of-the-poet

The Year of the Poet IV
May 2017

The Flowering Dogwood Tree

Featured Poets
Kallisa Powell
Alicja Maria Kuberska
Fethi Sassi

The Poetry Posse 2017

Gail Weston Shazor * Caroline Nazareno * Hussey Mohanty
Teresa E. Gallion * Anna Jakubczak Vel Ratty Adalan
Joe DaVerbal Minddancer * Sharon Abbist * Raphael
Albert Carrasco * Kimberly Burnham * Elizabeth Castillo
Hulya N. Yilmaz * Faleeha Hassan * Jackie Davis Allen
Jen Walls * Nizar Sartawi * * William S. Peters, Sr.

The Year of the Poet IV
June 2017

Featured Poets
Eliza Segiet
Tze-Min Tsai
Abdulla Issa

The Linden Tree

The Poetry Posse 2017

The Year of the Poet IV
July 2017

Featured Poets
Anca Mihaela Bruma
Ibaa Ismail
Zvonko Taneski

The Oak Moon

The Poetry Posse 2017

The Year of the Poet IV
August 2017

Featured Poets
Jonathan Aquino
Kitty Hsu
Langley Shazor

The Hazelnut Tree

The Poetry Posse 2017

Gail Weston Shazor * Caroline Nazareno
Teresa E. Gallion * Anna Jakubczak Vel Ratty Adalan
Joe DaVerbal Minddancer * Sharon Abbist * Raphael
Albert Carrasco * Kimberly Burnham * Elizabeth Castillo
Hulya N. Yilmaz * Faleeha Hassan * Jackie Davis Allen
Jen Walls * Nizar Sartawi * * William S. Peters, Sr.

# Now Available

www.innerchildpress.com/the-year-of-the-poet

## The Year of the Poet IV
September 2017

Featured Poets

Martina Reisz Newberr
Ameer Nassir
Christine Fulco Nea
Robert Neal

The Elm Tree

The Poetry Posse 2017

Gail Weston Shazor * Caroline Nazareno * Bismay Mohanty
Teresa E. Gallion * Anna Jakubczak Vel Ratty Adalan
Joe DaVerbal Minddancer * Shareef Abdur – Rasheed
Albert Carrasco * Kimberly Burnham * Elizabeth Castillo
Hülya N. Yılmaz * Faleeha Hassan * Jackie Davis Allen
Jen Walls * Nizar Sartawi * * William S. Peters, Sr.

## The Year of the Poet IV
October 2017

Featured Poets

**Ahmed Abu Saleem**
**Nedal Al-Qaeim**
**Sadeddin Shahin**

The Black Walnut Tree

The Poetry Posse 2017

Gail Weston Shazor * Caroline Nazareno * Bismay Mohanty
Teresa E. Gallion * Anna Jakubczak Vel Ratty Adalan
Joe DaVerbal Minddancer * Shareef Abdur – Rasheed
Albert Carrasco * Kimberly Burnham * Elizabeth Castillo
Hülya N. Yılmaz * Faleeha Hassan * Jackie Davis Allen
Jen Walls * Nizar Sartawi * * William S. Peters, Sr.

## The Year of the Poet IV
November 2017

Featured Poets

Kay Peters
Alfreda D. Ghee
Gabriella Garofalo
Rosemary Cappello

The Tree of Life

The Poetry Posse 2017

Gail Weston Shazor * Caroline Nazareno * Bismay Mohanty
Teresa E. Gallion * Anna Jakubczak Vel Ratty Adalan
Joe DaVerbal Minddancer * Shareef Abdur – Rasheed
Albert Carrasco * Kimberly Burnham * Elizabeth Castillo
Hülya N. Yılmaz * Faleeha Hassan * Jackie Davis Allen
Jen Walls * Nizar Sartawi * William S. Peters, Sr.

## The Year of the Poet IV
December 2017

Featured Poets

Justice Clarke
Mariel M. Pabroa
Kiley Brown

The Fig Tree

The Poetry Posse 2017

Gail Weston Shazor * Caroline Nazareno * Bismay Mohanty
Teresa E. Gallion * Anna Jakubczak Vel Ratty Adalan
Joe DaVerbal Minddancer * Shareef Abdur – Rasheed
Albert Carrasco * Kimberly Burnham * Elizabeth Castillo
Hülya N. Yılmaz * Faleeha Hassan * Jackie Davis Allen
Jen Walls * Nizar Sartawi * William S. Peters, Sr.

## Now Available

www.innerchildpress.com/the-year-of-the-poet

The Year of the Poet V
January 2018
Featured Poets
Iyad Shamasnah
Yasmeen Hamzeh
Ali Abdolrezaei

Aksum

The Poetry Posse 2018
Gail Weston Shazor * Caroline Nazareno * Tezmin Ition Tsai
Hülya N. Yılmaz * Faleeha Hassan * Jackie Davis Allen
Teresa E. Gallion * Anna Jakubczak Vel Ratty Adalan
Alicja Maria Kuberska * Shareef Abdur – Rasheed
Kimberly Burnham * Elizabeth Castillo
Nizar Sartawi * William S. Peters, Sr.

The Year of the Poet V
February 2018

Sabean

Featured Poets
Muhammad Azram
Anna Szawracka
Abhilipsa Kuanar
Aanika Aery

The Poetry Posse 2018
Gail Weston Shazor * Caroline Nazareno * Tezmin Ition Tsai
Hülya N. Yılmaz * Faleeha Hassan * Jackie Davis Allen
Teresa E. Gallion * Anna Jakubczak Vel Ratty Adalan
Alicja Maria Kuberska * Shareef Abdur – Rasheed
Kimberly Burnham * Elizabeth Castillo
Nizar Sartawi * William S. Peters, Sr.

The Year of the Poet V
March 2018

Featured Poets
Irum Fatima 'Ashi'
Cassandra Swan
Jaleel Khazaal
Shazia Zaman

Mexico
Cuba

Caribbean
&
Middle America

The Poetry Posse 2018
Gail Weston Shazor * Nizar Sartawi * Hülya N. Yılmaz
Jackie Davis Allen * Caroline 'Ceri' Nazareno
Alicja Maria Kuberska * Teresa E. Gallion
Faleeha Hassan * Shareef Abdur – Rasheed
Kimberly Burnham * Elizabeth Castillo
Tezmin Ition Tsai * William S. Peters, Sr.

The Year of the Poet V
April 2018

Featured Poets

The Nez Perce

The Poetry Posse 2018

*Now Available*

www.innerchildpress.com/the-year-of-the-poet

The Year of the Poet V
May 2018

Featured Poets
Zaddy Carreon de León Jr.
Kulwant K. Malinowska
Landita Alonzo
Ofelia Produn

The Sumerians

The Poetry Posse 2018

Gail Weston Shazor * Nizar Sartawi * Hülya N. Yılmaz
Jackie Davis Allen * Caroline 'Ceri' Nazareno
Alicja Maria Kuberska * Teresa E. Gallion
Kimberly Burnham * Shareef Abdur – Rasheed
Faleeha Hassan * Elizabeth Castillo * Swapna Behera
Tezmin Ition Tsai * William S. Peters, Sr.

The Year of the Poet V
June 2018

Featured Poets
Bilall Maliqi * Daun Mihari * Gojko Božović * Sofija Živković

The Paleo Indians

The Poetry Posse 2018

Gail Weston Shazor * Nizar Sartawi * Hülya N. Yılmaz
Jackie Davis Allen * Caroline 'Ceri' Nazareno
Alicja Maria Kuberska * Teresa E. Gallion
Kimberly Burnham * Shareef Abdur – Rasheed
Faleeha Hassan * Elizabeth Castillo * Swapna Behera
Tezmin Ition Tsai * William S. Peters, Sr.

The Year of the Poet V
July 2018

Featured Poets
Raphael Drogue-Paddy
Mohammad Ikbal Hath
Eliza Segiet
Tom Higgins

Oceania

The Poetry Posse 2018

Gail Weston Shazor * Nizar Sartawi * Hülya N. Yılmaz
Jackie Davis Allen * Caroline 'Ceri' Nazareno
Alicja Maria Kuberska * Teresa E. Gallion
Kimberly Burnham * Shareef Abdur – Rasheed
Faleeha Hassan * Elizabeth Castillo * Swapna Behera
Tezmin Ition Tsai * William S. Peters, Sr.

The Year of the Poet V
August 2018

Featured Poets
Hussein Habasch * Mircea Dan Duta * Naida Mujkić * Swagat Das

The Lapita

The Poetry Posse 2018

Gail Weston Shazor * Nizar Sartawi * Hülya N. Yılmaz
Jackie Davis Allen * Caroline 'Ceri' Nazareno
Alicja Maria Kuberska * Teresa E. Gallion
Kimberly Burnham * Shareef Abdur – Rasheed
Ashok K. Bhargava* Elizabeth Castillo * Swapna Behaera
Tezmin Ition Tsai * William S. Peters, Sr

*Now Available*

www.innerchildpress.com/the-year-of-the-poet

## The Year of the Poet V
September 2018

### The Aztecs & Incas

**Featured Poets**
Kolade Olanrewaju Freedom
Eliza Segiet
Mashet Hossain Abdul Ghani
Lily Swarn

The Poetry Posse 2018

Gail Weston Shazor * Nizar Sartawi * Hülya N. Yılmaz
Jackie Davis Allen * Caroline 'Ceri' Nazareno
Alicja Maria Kubenka * Teresa E. Gallion
Kimberly Burnham * Shareef Abdur – Rasheed
Ashok K. Bhargava * Elizabeth Castillo * Swapna Behera
Tezmin Ition Tsai * William S. Peters, Sr.

## The Year of the Poet V
October 2018

**Featured Poets**
Alicia Minjarez * Lonneice Weeks-Badley
Lopamudra Mishra * Abdelwahed Souayah

The Poetry Posse 2018

Gail Weston Shazor * Nizar Sartawi * Hülya N. Yılmaz
Jackie Davis Allen * Caroline 'Ceri' Nazareno
Alicja Maria Kubenka * Teresa E. Gallion
Kimberly Burnham * Shareef Abdur – Rasheed
Ashok K. Bhargava * Elizabeth Castillo * Swapna Behera
Tezmin Ition Tsai * William S. Peters, Sr.

## The Year of the Poet V
November 2018

**Featured Poets**
Michelle Joan Barulich * Monsif Beroual
Krystyna Konecka * Nassira Nezzar

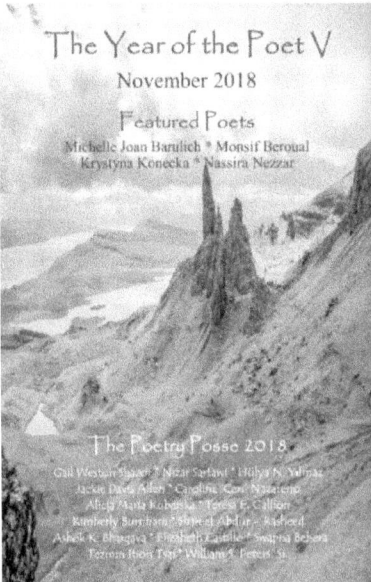

The Poetry Posse 2018

Gail Weston Shazor * Nizar Sartawi * Hülya N. Yılmaz
Jackie Davis Allen * Caroline 'Ceri' Nazareno
Alicja Maria Kubenka * Teresa E. Gallion
Kimberly Burnham * Shareef Abdur – Rasheed
Ashok K. Bhargava * Elizabeth Castillo * Swapna Behera
Tezmin Ition Tsai * William S. Peters, Sr.

## The Year of the Poet V
December 2018

**Featured Poets**
Rose Terranova Cirigliano
Joanna Kalinowska
Sokolović Emin
Dr. T. Ashok Chakravarthy

The Poetry Posse 2018

Gail Weston Shazor * Nizar Sartawi * Hülya N. Yılmaz
Jackie Davis Allen * Caroline 'Ceri' Nazareno
Alicja Maria Kubenka * Teresa E. Gallion
Kimberly Burnham * Shareef Abdur – Rasheed
Ashok K. Bhargava * Elizabeth Castillo * Swapna Behera
Tezmin Ition Tsai * William S. Peters, Sr.

## Now Available

www.innerchildpress.com/the-year-of-the-poet

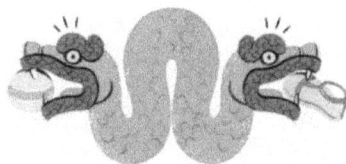

## The Year of the Poet VI

May 2019

Featured Poets

Emad Al-Haydary * Hussein Nasser Jabr
Wahab Sheriff * Abdul Razzaq Al Ameeri

Asia Southeast Asia and Maritime Asia

The Poetry Posse 2019

Gail Weston Shazor * Albert Carrasco * Hülya N. Yılmaz
Jackie Davis Allen * Caroline Nazareno * Eliza Segiet
Alicja Maria Kubenska * Teresa E. Gallion * Joe Paire
Kimberly Burnham * Shareef Abdur - Rasheed
Ashok K. Bhargava * Elizabeth Castillo * Swapna Behera
Tezmin Ition Tsai * William S. Peters, Sr.

## The Year of the Poet VI

June 2019

Featured Poets

Kate Gaudi Powiekszone * Sahaj Sabharwal
Iwu Jeff * Mohamed Abdel Aziz Shmeis

Arctic
Circumpolar

The Poetry Posse 2019

Gail Weston Shazor * Albert Carrasco * Hülya N. Yılmaz
Jackie Davis Allen * Caroline Nazareno * Eliza Segiet
Alicja Maria Kubenska * Teresa E. Gallion * Joe Paire
Kimberly Burnham * Shareef Abdur - Rasheed
Ashok K. Bhargava * Elizabeth Castillo * Swapna Behera
Tezmin Ition Tsai * William S. Peters, Sr.

## The Year of the Poet VI

Featured Poets

Saadeddin Shahin * Andy Scott
Fahreddin Sheku * Alok Kumar Ray

The Horn of Africa

Ethiopia          Djibouti

Somalia          Eritrea

The Poetry Posse 2019

Gail Weston Shazor * Albert Carrasco * Hülya N. Yılmaz
Jackie Davis Allen * Caroline Nazareno * Eliza Segiet
Alicja Maria Kubenska * Teresa E. Gallion * Joe Paire
Kimberly Burnham * Shareef Abdur - Rasheed
Ashok K. Bhargava * Elizabeth Castillo * Swapna Behera
Tezmin Ition Tsai * William S. Peters, Sr.

## The Year of the Poet VI

August 2019

Featured Poets

Shola Balogun * Bharati Nayak
Monalisa Dash Dwibedy * Mbizo  Chirasha

Coexist

Southwest Asia

The Poetry Posse 2019

Gail Weston Shazor * Albert Carrasco * Hülya N. Yılmaz
Jackie Davis Allen * Caroline Nazareno * Eliza Segiet
Alicja Maria Kubenska * Teresa E. Gallion * Joe Paire
Kimberly Burnham * Shareef Abdur - Rasheed
Ashok K. Bhargava * Elizabeth Castillo * Swapna Behera
Tezmin Ition Tsai * William S. Peters, Sr.

## Now Available

www.innerchildpress.com/the-year-of-the-poet

## The Year of the Poet VI
### September 2019

Featured Poets

Elena Liliana Popescu * Gobinda Biswas
Iram Fatima "Ashi" * Joseph S. Spence, Sr.

The Caucasus

The Poetry Posse 2019

Gail Weston Shazor * Albert Carrasco * Hülya N. Yilmaz
Jackie Davis Allen * Caroline Nazareno * Eliza Segiet
Alicja Maria Kubenska * Teresa E. Gallion * Joe Paire
Kimberly Burnham * Shareef Abdur – Rasheed
Ashok K. Bhargava * Elizabeth Castillo * Swapna Behera
Tezmin Ition Tsai * William S. Peters, Sr.

## The Year of the Poet VI
### October 2019

Featured Poets

Ngozi Olivia Osuoha * Denisa Kondži
Pankhuri Sinha * Christena AV Williams

The Nile Valley

The Poetry Posse 2019

Gail Weston Shazor * Albert Carrasco * Hülya N. Yilmaz
Jackie Davis Allen * Caroline Nazareno * Eliza Segiet
Alicja Maria Kubenska * Teresa E. Gallion * Joe Paire
Kimberly Burnham * Shareef Abdur – Rasheed
Ashok K. Bhargava * Elizabeth Castillo * Swapna Behera
Tezmin Ition Tsai * William S. Peters, Sr.

## The Year of the Poet VI
### November 2019

Featured Poets

Rozalia Aleksandrova * Orlendo Ganga
Seenati Ranjan Mohanty * Sofia Skleida

Northern Asia

The Poetry Posse 2019

Gail Weston Shazor * Albert Carrasco * Hülya N. Yilmaz
Jackie Davis Allen * Caroline Nazareno * Eliza Segiet
Alicja Maria Kubenska * Teresa E. Gallion * Joe Paire
Kimberly Burnham * Shareef Abdur – Rasheed
Ashok K. Bhargava * Elizabeth Castillo * Swapna Behera
Tezmin Ition Tsai * William S. Peters, Sr.

## The Year of the Poet VI
### December 2019

Featured Poets

Bilton Karlmi Karowei * Sujata Paul
Bharात Nayak * Kapardeli Dikcha

Oceania

The Poetry Posse 2019

Gail Weston Shazor * Albert Carrasco * Hülya N. Yilmaz
Jackie Davis Allen * Caroline Nazareno * Eliza Segiet
Alicja Maria Kubenska * Teresa E. Gallion * Joe Paire
Kimberly Burnham * Shareef Abdur – Rasheed
Ashok K. Bhargava * Elizabeth Castillo * Swapna Behera
Tezmin Ition Tsai * William S. Peters, Sr.

## Now Available

www.innerchildpress.com/the-year-of-the-poet

## The Year of the Poet VII
### January 2020

Featured Poets

B S Tyagi * Ashok Chakravarthy Tholana
Andy Scott * Anwer Ghani

1901 Jean Henry Dunant and Frédéric Passy

The Year of Peace
Celebrating past Nobel Peace Prize Recipients

The Poetry Posse 2020

Gail Weston Shazor * Albert Carasico * Hülya N. Yilmaz
Jackie Davis Allen * Caroline Nazareno * Eliza Segiet
Alicja Maria Kuberska * Teresa E. Gallion * Joe Paire
Kimberly Burnham * Shareef Abdur – Rasheed
Ashok K. Bhargava * Elizabeth Castillo * Swapna Behera
Tezmin Ition Tsai * William S. Peters, Sr.

## The Year of the Poet VII
### February 2020

Featured Poets

Jennifer Ades * Martina Reisz Newberry
Ibrahim Honjo * Claudia Piccinno

Henri La Fontaine ~ 1913

The Year of Peace
Celebrating past Nobel Peace Prize Recipients

The Poetry Posse 2020

Gail Weston Shazor * Albert Carasico * Hülya N. Yilmaz
Jackie Davis Allen * Caroline Nazareno * Eliza Segiet
Alicja Maria Kuberska * Teresa E. Gallion * Joe Paire
Kimberly Burnham * Shareef Abdur – Rasheed
Ashok K. Bhargava * Elizabeth Castillo * Swapna Behera
Tezmin Ition Tsai * William S. Peters, Sr.

## The Year of the Poet VII
### March 2020

Featured Poets

Aziz Mountassir * Krishna Paraisa
Hannie Rouweler * Rozalia Aleksandrova

Aristide Briand ~ 1926 ~ Gustav Stresemann

The Year of Peace
Celebrating past Nobel Peace Prize Recipients

The Poetry Posse 2020

Gail Weston Shazor * Albert Carasico * Hülya N. Yilmaz
Jackie Davis Allen * Caroline Nazareno * Eliza Segiet
Alicja Maria Kuberska * Teresa E. Gallion * Joe Paire
Kimberly Burnham * Shareef Abdur – Rasheed
Ashok K. Bhargava * Elizabeth Castillo * Swapna Behera
Tezmin Ition Tsai * William S. Peters, Sr.

## The Year of the Poet VII
### April 2020

Featured Poets

Rohini Behera * Mrteen Dan Duta
Monalisa Dash Dwibedy * NilavroNill Shoovro

Carlos Saavedra Lamas ~ 1936

The Year of Peace
Celebrating past Nobel Peace Prize Recipients

The Poetry Posse 2020

Gail Weston Shazor * Albert Carasico * Hülya N. Yilmaz
Jackie Davis Allen * Caroline Nazareno * Eliza Segiet
Alicja Maria Kuberska * Teresa E. Gallion * Joe Paire
Kimberly Burnham * Shareef Abdur – Rasheed
Ashok K. Bhargava * Elizabeth Castillo * Swapna Behera
Tezmin Ition Tsai * William S. Peters, Sr.

## Now Available

www.innerchildpress.com/the-year-of-the-poet

The Year of the Poet VII
May 2020

Featured Poets
Alok Kumar Ray * Eden S. Trinidad
Franco Barbato * Izabela Zubko

Ralph Bunche ~ 1950

The Year of Peace
Celebrating past Nobel Peace Prize Recipients

The Poetry Posse 2020

Gail Weston Shazor * Albert Carasico * Hülya N. Yılmaz
Jackie Davis Allen * Caroline Nazareno * Eliza Segiet
Alicja Maria Kuberska * Teresa E. Gallion * Joe Paire
Kimberly Burnham * Shareef Abdur – Rasheed
Ashok K. Bhargava * Elizabeth Castillo * Swapna Behera
Tezmin Ition Tsai * William S. Peters, Sr.

The Year of the Poet VII
June 2020

Featured Poets
Eftichia Kapardeli * Metin Cengiz
Hussein Habasch * Kosh K Mathew

Albert John Lutuli ~ 1960

The Year of Peace
Celebrating past Nobel Peace Prize Recipients

The Poetry Posse 2020

Gail Weston Shazor * Albert Carasico * Hülya N. Yılmaz
Jackie Davis Allen * Caroline Nazareno * Eliza Segiet
Alicja Maria Kuberska * Teresa E. Gallion * Joe Paire
Kimberly Burnham * Shareef Abdur – Rasheed
Ashok K. Bhargava * Elizabeth Castillo * Swapna Behera
Tezmin Ition Tsai * William S. Peters, Sr.

The Year of the Poet VII
July 2020

Featured Poets
Mykola Martyniuk * Orbindu Ganga
Roula Pollard * Karri Praktisha

Norman Ernest Borlaug ~ 1970

The Year of Peace
Celebrating past Nobel Peace Prize Recipients

The Poetry Posse 2020

Gail Weston Shazor * Albert Carasico * Hülya N. Yılmaz
Jackie Davis Allen * Caroline Nazareno * Eliza Segiet
Alicja Maria Kuberska * Teresa E. Gallion * Joe Paire
Kimberly Burnham * Shareef Abdur – Rasheed
Ashok K. Bhargava * Elizabeth Castillo * Swapna Behera
Tezmin Ition Tsai * William S. Peters, Sr.

The Year of the Poet VII
August 2020

Featured Poets
Dr Pragya Suman * Chinh Nguyen
Srinivas Vasudev * Ugwu Leonard Ifeanyi, Jr.

Adolfo Pérez Esquivel ~ 1980

The Year of Peace
Celebrating past Nobel Peace Prize Recipients

The Poetry Posse 2020

Gail Weston Shazor * Albert Carasico * Hülya N. Yılmaz
Jackie Davis Allen * Caroline Nazareno * Eliza Segiet
Alicja Maria Kuberska * Teresa E. Gallion * Joe Paire
Kimberly Burnham * Shareef Abdur – Rasheed
Ashok K. Bhargava * Elizabeth Castillo * Swapna Behera
Tezmin Ition Tsai * William S. Peters, Sr.

## Now Available

www.innerchildpress.com/the-year-of-the-poet

201

The Year of the Poet VII

September 2020

Featured Poets

Raed Anis Al-Jishi • Soleiconvie Steckane
Dr. Brajesh Kumar Gupta • Umid Najjari

**Mikhail Sergeyevich Gorbachev ~ 1990**

The Year of Peace
Celebrating past Nobel Peace Prize Recipients

The Poetry Posse 2020

Gail Weston Shazor • Albert Carrasco • Hülya N. Yılmaz
Jackie Davis Allen • Caroline Nazareno • Eliza Segiet
Alicja Maria Kuberska • Teresa E. Gallion • Joe Paire
Kimberly Burnham • Shareef Abdur - Rasheed
Ashok K. Bhargava • Elizabeth Castillo • Swapna Behera
Tezmin Ition Tsai • William S. Peters, Sr.

The Year of the Poet VII

October 2020

Featured Poets

Mutawaf A. Shaheed • Galina Italyanskaya
Nadeem Fraz • Avril Tanya Meallem

**Kim Dae-jung ~ 2000**

The Year of Peace
Celebrating past Nobel Peace Prize Recipients

The Poetry Posse 2020

Gail Weston Shazor • Albert Carrasco • Hülya N. Yılmaz
Jackie Davis Allen • Caroline Nazareno • Eliza Segiet
Alicja Maria Kuberska • Teresa E. Gallion • Joe Paire
Kimberly Burnham • Shareef Abdur - Rasheed
Ashok K. Bhargava • Elizabeth Castillo • Swapna Behera
Tezmin Ition Tsai • William S. Peters, Sr.

The Year of the Poet VII

November 2020

Featured Poets

Elisa Mascia • Sue Lindenberg McClelland
Hatif Janabi • Ivan Gácina

**Liu Xiaobo ~ 2010**

The Year of Peace
Celebrating past Nobel Peace Prize Recipients

The Poetry Posse 2020

Gail Weston Shazor • Albert Carrasco • Hülya N. Yılmaz
Jackie Davis Allen • Caroline Nazareno • Eliza Segiet
Alicja Maria Kuberska • Teresa E. Gallion • Joe Paire
Kimberly Burnham • Shareef Abdur - Rasheed
Ashok K. Bhargava • Elizabeth Castillo • Swapna Behera
Tezmin Ition Tsai • William S. Peters, Sr.

# Now Available

www.innerchildpress.com/the-year-of-the-poet

and there is much, much more !

visit . . .

www.innerchildpress.com/antho
logies-sales-special.php

Also check out our Authors and
all the wonderful Books
Available at :

www.innerchildpress.com/autho
rs-pages

# World Healing World Peace
## 2020

# Poets for Humanity

## Now Available

www.worldhealingworldpeacepoetry.com

Now Available

205

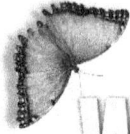

Support a

World Healing
World Peace

www.worldhealingworldpeacepoetry.com

World Healing
World Peace
2012, 2014, 2016, 2018, 2020

*Now Available*

www.worldhealingworldpeacepoetry.com

# Inner Child Press International

*'building bridges of cultural understanding'*

## Meet the Board of Directors

www.innerchildpress.com

# Inner Child Press International

*'building bridges of cultural understanding'*

## Meet our Cultural Ambassadors

Fahredin Shehu
Director of Cultural

Faleha Hassan
Iraq – USA

Elizabeth E. Castillo
Philippines

Antoinette Coleman
Chicago
Midwest USA

Ananda Nepali
Nepali Tribe
Northern India

Kimberly Burnham
Pacific Northwest
USA

Alicja Kuberska
Poland
Eastern Europe

Swapna Behera
India
Southeast Asia

Kolade O. Freedom
Nigeria
West Africa

Monsif Beroual
Morocco
Northern Africa

Ashok K. Bhargava
Canada

Teronin Ition Tsai
Republic of China
Greater China

Alicia M. Ramírez
Mexico
Central America

Christena AV Williams
Jamaica
Caribbean

Louise Hudon
Eastern Canada

Aziz Mountassir
Morocco
Northern Africa

Shareef Abdur-Rasheed
Southeastern USA

Laure Charazac
France
Western Europe

Mohammad Ikbal Harb
Lebanon
Middle East

Mohamed Abdel
Aziz Shmeis
Egypt
Middle East

Hillary Mainga
Kenya
Eastern Africa

Josephus R. Johnson
Liberia

## www.innerchildpress.com

This Anthological Publication
is underwritten solely by

*Inner Child Press International*

Inner Child Press is a Publishing Company
Founded and Operated by Writers. Our
personal publishing experiences provides
us an intimate understanding of the
sometimes daunting challenges Writers,
New and Seasoned may face in the
Business of Publishing and Marketing
their Creative "Written Work".

For more Information

*Inner Child Press International*

www.innerchildpress.com

'building bridges of cultural understanding'

www.innerchildpress.com

202 Wiltree Court, State College, Pennsylvania 16801

~ fini ~

www.ingramcontent.com/pod-product-compliance
Lightning Source LLC
LaVergne TN
LVHW051046080426
835508LV00019B/1729